THE UNITED METHODIST FREE CHURCHES

THE UNITED METHODIST
FREE CHURCHES

A Study in Freedom

by

OLIVER A. BECKERLEGGE
M.A., Ph.D.

WIPF & STOCK · Eugene, Oregon

Wipf and Stock Publishers
199 W 8th Ave, Suite 3
Eugene, OR 97401

The United Methodist Free Churches
A Study in Freedom
By Beckerlegge, Oliver A.
Copyright©1957 Methodist Publishing - Epworth Press
ISBN 13: 978-1-5326-3834-3
Publication date 7/27/2017
Previously published by Epworth Press, 1957

PREFACE

THE PREPARATION of this sketch has been a labour of love; and I would like, at the outset, to record my appreciation of the honour conferred on me by the Wesley Historical Society in asking me to undertake it. To many, the United Methodist Free Churches are not even a name; as a separate denomination, they had their day and ceased to be half a century ago, and Time is a terrible obliterator as well as a greater healer.

Strange as it may seem, the Free Methodists have never had their chronicler; Matthew Baxter wrote his *Memorials of Free Methodism*, but the denomination was only eight years old when he wrote, in 1865; and although Joseph Kirsop's *Historic Sketches* appeared twenty years later, that work was virtually a reprint of articles he contributed to the *Sheffield Independent* in July 1876. The fact that this is the first sketch of the whole half-century of their history must be the justification for its length.

In it I have striven to show not only the historical outlines of the Free Methodists, but something also of their ethos. Many of the principles for which they stood are under a cloud in these days; but some of us believe they are of eternal validity. Indeed there are some strange parallels with, and therefore pertinent commentaries on, events in very recent Methodist history, and the discerning eye will not fail to notice them!

In the preparation I have received help from many friends, and it is a pleasure to acknowledge my debt here to the Rev. J. Henry Martin and Dr Frank H. Cumbers; to the Revs. Norman P. Goldhawk, M.A., Walter Crow Hope, and the late Walter B. Hoult, M.A., B.D., to the late Mr Stephen J. Gee, Messrs R. S. Wainwright, J. L. Spedding and E. C. Cryer; and to the Rev W. T. Anderson, who drew my attention to E. R. Taylor's *Methodism and Politics, 1791-1851* (C.U.P., 1935), too late, unfortunately,

7

for me to be able to make use of it. Too late, too, for in-clusion in the body of the sketch, Mr Anderson told me the following anecdote which perfectly illustrates the sturdy independence of the Free Methodists:

When I was received into full Connexion I was 'sent' to Hol-beach. The minimum salary had just been raised from £100 to £110 and such circuits as were unable to raise the extra £10 could draw upon a Sustentation Fund. Holbeach was such a circuit, but being good Free Methodists hated to do so.

Shortly after my settling down I established a Circuit Magazine and at the end of a year revealed (what I had kept as a close secret) that I had a profit of £8 10s. for the circuit. Mr Robert Merry, J.P., Circuit Steward, moved a vote of thanks to me and suggested a collection there and then for the remaining £1 10s. so that they could free themselves from debt; that was done and the Doxology sung. They were now no longer an 'aided' circuit!

I am grateful also to Mrs J. W. Longstaff for the two sketch-maps that show at a glance where the strength of the United Methodist Free Churches lay geographically; and to the Rev. C. H. Rose, Lady Hosie, and Messrs Geo. F. Galpin and Alan Duckworth for the loan of photographs. But in these days of heavy printing costs, the inclusion of these maps, together with the other illus-trations, has been possible only because of the generous subventions of several Methodists (who wish to remain anonymous) with strong UMFC connexions; to these friends I am especially grateful. And, like all students of Methodist history, I am indebted to the Rev. Dr Frank Baker who read through the typescript, spending far more time on it than he ought to have done, and thereby saving me, by his judicious observations, from more infelicities of style and comment than I care to remember!

All these have helped me. Whatever of good the sketch contains is in some measure theirs; but the faults are my own.

OLIVER A. BECKERLEGGE

CONTENTS

I

ORIGINS

THE YEAR 1957 is a triple anniversary. It is of course the Silver Jubilee of Methodist Union in 1932; and that fact is not being forgotten connexionally. It is the Golden Jubilee of the Union of 1907, when the Bible Christians, the Methodist New Connexion, and the United Methodist Free Churches came together to form the United Methodist Church, a union that in many ways heralded, and paved the way for, the larger union of 1932. But it is also the Centenary of the union in 1857 which combined the Wesleyan Methodist Association and the bulk of the Wesleyan Reformers to form the United Methodist Free Churches; 1857 was the year of the first *rapprochement* of any considerable consequence after the disastrous splits of the previous sixty years. It is therefore an anniversary worth celebrating, not only because a Connexion came into existence then, but even more because it was the beginning of a new and historic trend in Methodism.

Who were these people—and what was it that brought them together? For one of the two strands of the rope that was called the United Methodist Free Churches was itself an association of smaller Connexions. In the first place there were the Protestant Methodists, who apparently had seceded[1] from parent Methodism because they did not want an organ in Brunswick Chapel, Leeds; there were the Arminian Methodists in and about Derby, who apparently had seceded on a question of doctrine; there were the Independent Primitive Methodists of Scarborough; there were the Welsh Independent Methodists; there were the Temperance Methodists of Cornwall; and

[1] The word 'seceded' has been used for simplicity's sake. In point of fact, very many were expelled, and the rest moved away simply to prevent their expulsion.

there were the circuits of the Wesleyan Association, who seceded or were expelled apparently because they objected to the establishment of a Theological Institution. Such a variety of causes would, one would think, make strange bed-fellows; but in every case there was a deeper underlying cause. Organs and institutions, temperance principles, and Sandemanian doctrine, were only the occasions; the cause in every case was the rights of local Methodism, or of private individuals, against central authority.

It is unnecessary to point out that all these disputes and disruptions took place at a time when political life was in a ferment throughout Britain and, indeed, Europe; it would be idle to deny that they were not unconnected with that fact—thus the troubles of 1827 and 1834 coincided with the agitation for, and the passing of, the Reform Bill of 1832; the later and greater troubles leading up to the disaster of 1849 coincided with the 'year of revolutions', 1848, and the Chartist agitation. But it is easy to overstress the connexion. Methodists there no doubt were who were primarily politicians—Joseph Rayner Stephens is a case in point—but it is a fair guess that the vast bulk of Methodists were primarily evangelical, Protestant Christians; and their political activity, when it existed, was simply the expression of one of the tenets of their faith: the Priesthood of All Believers. They took that doctrine seriously, and developed it. The Vice-President of the 1955 Conference warned us in his Address against importing words of political connotation, such as 'democracy', into the vocabulary of the Christian Church; political concepts had not necessarily any place in Christian Church life and thought. That is of course a half-truth; it is no use our stressing, as we do, that the early Trade Unionists and Labour leaders learned their belief in the value of the ordinary man through their connexion with Methodism, and then denying that those principles that they first learnt in Methodism, and later applied to their public life, have no place in Methodism! For want of a better word (and the Reformers of 1827 to 1849 used this word),

it was for 'democracy', the government of the Church,
locally or connexionally, by the rank and file of the membership exercising their priesthood, that the Reformers
struggled and suffered.

It will be inevitable, in telling the story of the United
Methodist Free Churches, to bring to light again

> *old, unhappy, far off things,*
> *And battles long ago.*

Comparisons must be drawn between the Reformers and
Wesleyan officials, often to the disparagement of the
latter (for the writer is convinced that the Reformers were
usually right). But let no one think that this study is the
fruit of blind prejudice against the former Wesleyan
Church; the writer has received far too much from ex-
Wesleyan saints for that to be so—'I am debtor both to
the Greeks, and to the barbarians; both to the wise, and
to the unwise.' The telling of history demands a fearless
recital of the facts as far as they can be discerned, an
attempt to see things through the eyes of the people
involved, and as honest an interpretation of them as
human fallibility can allow:

> *nothing extenuate,*
> *Nor set down aught in malice.*

From the death of Wesley, as is well known, there had
been demands for a larger measure of 'democracy' in the
life of the Church. The secessions and expulsions that led
to the formation of the Methodist New Connexion in
1797 were some of the offshoots of this agitation; the Plan
of Pacification in 1795 and the Leeds Concessions of 1797
were others. As the first Reformers all took their stand
on these two pronouncements, it will be well to quote the
relevant paragraphs:

It has been our general custom never to appoint or remove a
leader or steward without first consulting the leaders and
stewards of the society, and we are resolved to walk by the
same rule. (*Plan of Pacification*, Addenda (4).)

III. 1. The leaders' meeting shall have a right to declare any person on trial, improper to be received into the society; and, after such declaration, the superintendent shall not admit such person into the society.

2. No person shall be expelled from the society for immorality, till such immorality be proved at a leaders' meeting.

IV. In respect to the appointment and removal of leaders, stewards, and local preachers, and concerning meetings:

1. No person shall be appointed a leader or steward, or be removed from his office, but in conjunction with the leaders' meeting; the nomination to be in the superintendent, and the approbation or disapprobation in the leaders' meeting.

VI. We have determined that all the rules which relate to the societies, leaders, stewards, local preachers, trustees, and quarterly meetings, shall be published with the rules of the Society for the benefit and convenience of all the members.

. . . Thus, brethren, we have given up the greatest part of our executive government into your hands, as represented in your different public meetings.

5. There is now no society officer among us who can be received without the consent of that meeting to which he particularly belongs: nor can any officer be appointed, except upon the same plan. (*Leeds Concessions.*)[2]

The first secession with which we have to do concerns the Protestant Methodists. It was proposed to put an organ in Brunswick Chapel, Leeds, but when the question came before the leaders' meeting, the proposal was rejected by sixty votes to one. Whether the trustees were acting legally in then going to the District Meeting to ask permission seems obscure; Thomas Stanley, the superintendent of the circuit, had ruled 'that the concurrence of the leaders' meeting was necessary to success, and that without it the Conference would not listen to an application from any quarter whatever on the subject'.[3] Legal or not, they were certainly ill-advised, and it was

[2] As 'received' and 'appointed' signify the same thing, the former word is presumably a misprint for 'removed'.

[3] Matthew Johnson, 'Recollections of Leeds Methodism', in *UMFC Magazine* (1863), p. 288.

not surprising that the District Meeting, by a large majority, resolved that 'it was not desirable to grant the required permission to place an organ in Brunswick Chapel'.[4] There the matter should have rested, for the latest Conference ruling on organs, published in 1820, ran: 'Organs may be allowed by special consent of the Conference, but every application shall be first made to the District Meeting, and if it obtain their sanction, shall then be referred to a committee of the Conference.' Now, whatever this may be *made* to mean, the plain interpretation is that if such an application did not receive the sanction of the District Meeting, the matter could go no farther. But the trustees were determined to have their way, and so, by lobbying in the interval between the District Meeting and Conference, and by winning the ear of Jabez Bunting and other influential men at Conference, including the incoming President, they won their point. Conference unwisely ignored the superintendent's protests, the deliberate judgement of both leaders' meeting and District Meeting, and its own law, and gave the required permission.

But that, while it annoyed intensely the Brunswick leaders, caused no secessions. What angered them still more than the installation of the organ was what followed the Conference decision. An appeal was made to the incoming superintendent of the circuit to stay the operation of Conference's decision till an amicable arrangement could be made. This he declined to do, not feeling it in his power to interfere. A local preacher, Matthew Johnson, summoned the local preachers of the two Leeds circuits together—an illegal proceeding—to protest against Conference's setting aside of its own laws. For this he was first suspended from the exercise of his office, then expelled. But seventy local preachers sided with him, and the superintendent, who was also Chairman of the District, had recourse to a Special District Meeting, whose constitution, as laid down in the *Leeds Concessions* of 1797, was the incorporation of 'three of the nearest superintendents' with the

[4] ibid.

B

District Committee; the President could be invited at the discretion of the Chairman. Again, the law was sufficiently precise; but the harassed superintendent and chairman, instead of inviting 'three of the nearest superintendents', passed over the superintendents of such important circuits as Sheffield and Bradford, and went as far as Liverpool. And in addition to the President, John Stephens, who should be there but Jabez Bunting, in his specially created office of 'Official Adviser of the President'. One may guess that it was *not* John Stephens who invited him and appointed him to that office! This meeting confirmed the illegality of the meeting called by Johnson, but, forgetting that its purpose was to settle disputes and not to try offenders, proceeded to expel Johnson and his colleague James Sigston. It was at this Special District Meeting that Bunting coined perhaps his most famous Buntingism: 'Methodism knows nothing of democracy; Methodism hates democracy as it hates sin.' The matter came up again at the Conference of 1828 when there was considerable criticism of the handling of the case in the Special District Meeting, Richard Watson even going to the length of proposing that the permission to erect an organ should be suspended till the Conference of 1829 in order to find time for a real attempt at reconciling trustees, leaders, and local preachers. Then Bunting rose; he contended that if the Constitution had been strained and the law broken, it was justified by the grave emergency, for the question was ultimately one of 'an insurrection against the pastoral office'. Consequently he moved, and Conference resolved: 'That it is the judgement of the Conference that the Special District Meeting held in Leeds was both indispensably necessary, and, in the most extraordinary emergency, constitutional also.'

The upshot was the loss of a thousand members in the two Leeds circuits, and the formation of the Protestant Methodist Connexion, who held their first service in Ebenezer Methodist New Connexion Chapel in Leeds on Christmas Day 1827. Within a very short time, need was felt for a chapel to replace the various rooms in which the Protestants had worshipped; and when they were on the point of completing the purchase of a site on which to build, a disused Baptist Chapel in St Peter's Street holding 700 was offered for sale and was immediately purchased. In March 1828—within three months of their first service—this 'Stone Chapel' was reopened for public worship. This chapel deserves recording, since it was the first owned by any section of the United Methodist Free Churches. But the loss was not restricted to Leeds; secessions, to form Protestant Methodist societies, took place in many other towns—Barnsley, Burnley, Keighley, London, Preston, and Sheffield all had circuits which continued into the later Unions; no doubt there were secessions in other places of which trace has been lost.

We have told the story of this disruption at some length, as some of its features explain many of the principles underlying the life and thought of the United Methodist Free Churches. Time after time in the story we see Conference, or Conference officials, breaking their own rules— the allowing of the appeal to Conference after the District Meeting had refused permission to install the organ is a case in point; the breaking of the constitution of the Special District Meeting in order in obtain a 'packed committee' is another; the use of this meeting to try and expel members is a third. The UMFC were always very careful lest connexional rules should be broken; and one question which later arose in their Assemblies on a number of occasions was always settled by the question, *not* 'What can this law be made to mean?' but 'What was the original intention of those who framed this law, and how did they themselves interpret it in practice?' A law could be rescinded; but until it was rescinded it was the law, and not even Conference could break it. Says Gregory: 'It is a most perilous proceeding for the highest Church Court to take the initiative in irregularity. Against this Mr Bunting himself had faithfully forewarned the Conference some years before, in his golden axiom: "If *we* do not respect our laws, what wonder that our people

should not heed them!" '[5] Had Bunting always followed
his own dictum, the whole future history of Methodism
might have been different. But no; anything could be
considered constitutional 'in the most extraordinary
emergency'. Then again, members of the Leeds societies
were expelled by a meeting consisting partly of superintendents of other circuits; and to this fact can in part
be attributed the very strong feeling among the UMFC
that neither the Annual Assembly (as their Conference
was called) nor the itinerant preachers had authority 'to
suspend or expel any non-Itinerant, usually called Local
Preachers, Steward, Leader, or other member of the said
Association; the Circuit, Society, or Church meetings,
and authorities, constituted according to the custom or
rule of each such Circuit, possessing the exclusive power
of suspending and expelling all such persons'.[6] It was
unmistakably the arbitrary actions of Conference that
gave rise to the near-Congregationalism of the UMFC,
just as it was Bunting's excessive concern for the pastoral
office[7]—what the Reformers dubbed 'pastoral supremacy'
—that caused the very first Conference of the Wesleyan
Association to resolve that it was 'inexpedient that the
term "Reverend" should be used in connexion with the
name of any Preacher in the Association'.[8] This was
rescinded—presumably for practical reasons—nine years
later; but already in 1842 the title was slipping back into
use. Yet as late as 1876, William Griffith, one of the three
expelled in 1849, always one of the *enfants terribles* of the
UMFC (was not his effigy burnt in Derby Market place?),
introduced a motion to discountenance the use of the
term, which he himself never used; but after discussion
the motion was withdrawn.[9]

[5] Benjamin Gregory, *Sidelights on the Conflicts of Methodism* (London 1898), p. 52.

[6] Foundation Deed of the Wesleyan Methodist Association, clause 10 (pub. in *WMA Minutes*, 1840).

[7] cf. J. H. S. Kent, *Jabez Bunting, the last Wesleyan* (London 1955).

[8] *Minutes* (1836), p. 18.

[9] Silas K. Hocking also would not use the term; cf. his *My Book of Memory* (London 1923), p. 178.

The Wesleyan Association, the second group of importance, arose out of the proposal to establish a 'Theological
Institution'. It was at first sight strange that Methodists,
who have, at their best, always been concerned for self-
culture and the development of one's God-given faculties
to their fullest extent, should object to thorough training
for their preachers; just as it was surely strange that
Yorkshire Methodists—of all people!—should object to
the enhancement of the musical side of worship. James
Everett summed up the general feeling of unrest by
saying: 'All is dark; Methodism is ruined. I see in vision
the fine natural orator lost, and instead of a bold, hale,
original, and powerful ministry, there is the refined senti-
mentality of some other denominations—all form, all
system; a shadow of the past; the ghost of a Primitive
Methodist preacher—the moon in her frosty brightness,
instead of the sun going forth in his might.'[10] But the root
objection was at least as much to the manner of pressing
the proposal through Conference as to the proposal itself.
As with the Leeds Organ Case, the Institution was the
occasion rather than the underlying cause. What, in
brief, happened? The 1833 Conference appointed a committee, of which Bunting was a member, to arrange a plan
for the education of candidates for the Ministry. The
committee, as other committees sometimes have done,
went farther than its brief, and not only formulated the
scheme, but proceeded to nominate Jabez Bunting as
'President of the Theological Institution' and Theological
Tutor, in spite of the fact that he was already Missionary
Secretary, had twice been President of Conference, had
had two spells as Secretary, and was Convener of the
Stationing Committee. The scheme as thus put forward
was approved by the ensuing Conference of 1834, in
violation of the *Leeds Concessions* which required that 'no
regulation be finally confirmed till after a year's consideration, and the knowledge of the sentiments of the Connexion

[10] Letter to Dr Warren, dated 4th December 1834, quoted in Joseph
Kirsop, *Historic Sketches of Free Methodism* (London 1885), p. 27.

at large, through the medium of all their public officers'.[11]
There is no question but that the Conference of 1834 broke
the letter and spirit of the *Concessions* in at once determin-
ing on the establishment of the Theological Institution
without consulting the societies. Added to all this, there
was natural resentment that Bunting was to hold another
key office, and 'centralization' would be further strengthened by keeping Bunting in London.

Dr Samuel Warren led the opposition, though in the
committee, of which he was a member, he had approved
of the principle. It was when Dr Bunting's name was
coupled with the scheme that his opposition developed—
some have suggested unworthily, because he, Warren,
was a disappointed man. It is probably nearer to the
truth to say that his objection was genuinely to placing
increased power in one man's hands, whether that man
were Bunting or any other. He attacked the scheme soon
after Conference in a pamphlet, *Remarks on the Wesleyan
Theological Institution*,[12] which passed through several
editions, and for which he was suspended from his superintendency of the Manchester First Circuit by a Special
District Meeting. Unhappily he had recourse to the
Courts, asking that Oldham Street pulpit be restored to
him. Upon the Vice-Chancellor's rejecting his application, Warren appealed, and on 18th March 1835 and the
three succeeding days, his case was heard before Lord
Chancellor Lyndhurst, who upheld the previous decision.
This was followed a month later by a meeting in Manchester of delegates from all parts of the kingdom; for opposition to the scheme had been organized up and down the
country from the autumn following its acceptance by the
1834 Conference. Leading Laymen had been expelled in
Liverpool, Manchester, Hull, Rochdale, Sunderland,
Whitehaven, Birmingham, London, and other circuits.
In November 1834 a meeting had been held in Manchester at which the 'Grand Central Association' was formed.

[11] *Leeds Concessions*, Addendum, para. 6.
[12] It has been estimated that well-nigh a thousand pamphlets were published in the course of the Warrenite controversy.

Finally, in April 1835, upwards of a hundred delegates met and formulated their demands, which, summed up, were a demand for self-government in the circuits and representation in Conference. They met again in Sheffield at the same time as Conference was being held there, remaining in session a week and hoping that Conference would meet them; but their address was received by Conference with contempt. So far from meeting them, Conference expelled Warren, Robert Emmett (a supernumerary), and John Averill (the junior minister in Camelford, Cornwall) who had sided with the Reformers in the Camelford Circuit soon after the Manchester meeting the previous November.[13] (With Warren, Averill joined the Wesleyan Association in 1836, but withdrew in 1839.) The result was that the delegates issued their final appeal to the rank and file of the Methodist people, and the following year held their first Annual Assembly, in the interval having been joined by the Protestant Methodists. The first *Minutes* record no schedules of membership, but the following year they report 21,000 members. At this first Assembly Dr Warren was elected President, and Matthew Johnson, the leader of the Protestant Methodists, Secretary; there were four itinerant preachers present besides Dr Warren. Forty-two towns or circuits were represented, some by as many as twelve delegates; in addition nine others were represented by letters, and two brethren represented the 'Scottish Methodist Churches'. For in the interval between 1827 and 1836, movements for reform had spread throughout the length and breadth of the land; and while the majority of the places represented were in Lancashire, Yorkshire, and the Midlands,[14] so widespread had the feeling for reform grown—all summed up in a common protest against 'violations of Methodist law and infringements upon the rights and privileges of

[13] The story of Averill and what took place in Camelford is described in the *Wesley Historical Society Proceedings* (henceforward referred to as *WHS Proc.*), XXVIII.151ff.

[14] cf. *The Jubilee of the Methodist New Connexion* (London 1848), p. 354, for a note that the seceders in 1836 in Dudley and neighbourhood joined the MNC rather than the Wesleyan Association.

the Members of the Methodist Societies'[15]—that there were also brethren present from places as far afield as London, Camelford, Louth, Darlington, Carlisle, not to mention Edinburgh and Carrickfergus, and letters from places such as Plymouth and the Isle of Man, too far distant conveniently to send delegates. What probably did most to fan the incipient flames of revolt was an amazing discovery made by Dr Warren during the course of his Chancery suit; though one must not forget that the Leeds affair had repercussions as far as London itself. Dr Warren was advised by his Counsel to consult the *Journal* of Conference. John Mason the Book Steward twice refused him permission, and only granted it on threat of an immediate application to the Lord Chancellor;[16] Warren then discovered that neither the *Plan of Pacification* nor the *Leeds Concessions* had been entered in the *Journals*, which entry alone could give force to the law. This *may* have been accidental; but the reformers were in no mood for giving the authorities the benefit of the doubt, especially as the Secretary for 1795 (Dr Coke), who should have entered the *Plan of Pacification*, was the President for 1797 when the later omission took place. Needless to say, this dual omission was published on scores of platforms, and contributed not a little to the spread of revolt.

The first Assembly, then, was held on 3rd August 1836 and succeeding days, in the wooden Tabernacle, Stephenson Square, Manchester. It spent its time, roughly speaking, on four matters: a protest against the conduct of the 'Methodist Conference', the drawing-up of provisional regulations for the societies associated with it, an invitation to such other liberal branches of the Methodist family as showed themselves willing to join, and the supplying of preachers to circuits (though no 'Stations' appear in the printed *Minutes*). In pursuance of the third of these matters, brethren were appointed to visit the 'Yearly

---

[15] *Minutes* (1836), p. 6. Henceforward, all references to *Minutes*, unless otherwise stated, are to the *Wesleyan Methodist Association Minutes* (1836-56), and the *UMFC Minutes* (1857-1907). Similarly, references to *Magazine* are to the *UMFC Magazine*.

[16] Matthew Baxter, *Memorials of Free Methodism* (London 1865), p. 218.

Meeting' of the Protestant Methodists (though they had taken part in the proceedings of the Assembly, they clearly had not yet as a body formally become affiliated), various circuits of reformers who were not yet affiliated, and a group of dissidents in Scotland; it was to these dissidents that the Assembly sent its only 'Address' that year, and they were already in some measure organized as a body with a yearly meeting.

By the following Assembly, held in the Music Hall, Bold Street, Liverpool, invitations to amalgamate had been accepted by the Independent Primitive Methodists of Scarborough and their minister Matthew Baxter, by the Arminian Methodists and the Revs. Henry Breeden, Samuel Sellars, John Wright and three other ministers, and by an independent circuit in Sunderland whose minister was Thomas W. Pearson. The outlines of a constitution had been drafted by the previous Assembly and, having been under discussion in the societies during the year, were now finally worked out. It was in this Assembly that one of the guiding principles of the Wesleyan Association, and later of the UMFC, was fought out: the nature of the membership of the Annual Assembly. A number of representatives, headed by Dr Warren, stood for the plan of the New Connexion, by which each circuit elected one minister and one layman; the opposite party, headed by Robert Eckett of London, stood for free representation; and it was free representation, without any *ex officio* rights, that won the day. In consequence of his defeat in this battle royal—and a battle royal it was, by all accounts[17]—Dr Warren that autumn quitted the Association and became not, as one might logically have expected, a New Connexion Minister, but an Anglican one. Dr George Eayrs is perhaps a little harsh in his summing up: 'He travelled the country in exposition of some of the reforms and principles for which the Wesleyan Methodist Association contended, and was its first President; but when these principles came to be elaborated, he was unwilling to accept them';[18] and Cyril Davey is even

[17] cf. ibid. p. 442. [18] *Our Founders and Their Story* (London 1907), p. 27.

harsher, calling him 'a self-opinionated trouble-maker'.[19]
It does not follow necessarily that because Warren had
argued for reform, he wanted reform in the shape which
finally emerged; yet the fact remains that he was certainly
one of the less noble of the Reformers. He died in 1862.[20]

The Arminian Methodists had seceded, or been expelled,
in 1831 or 1832. Their separation has been described more
than once as constituting the only secession for doctrinal
reasons that ever took place within Methodism;[21] and,
curiously enough, they survive today (or at any rate did
in 1939) in Germany, where they are known as the *Bund
freikirchlicher Christen*, or, more popularly, the *Derbisten*.
But it may be doubted whether in fact their secession was
really on account of wrong teaching. They were charged
with holding 'Sandemanian views as to the nature of
saving faith';[22] it was said that they believed 'that faith
was human, not that they ignored the need of divine help,
but rather that they held that, the help having been given,
the seeking soul ought at once to believe'.[23] The doctrine
is stated thus on Robert Sandeman's tombstone: 'That
the bare death of Jesus Christ without a thought or deed
on the part of man is sufficient to present the chief of
sinners spotless before God'; so that justifying faith is
simple assent to the divine testimony concerning Jesus
Christ. It was all probably an argument about words.
They were ardent evangelicals and revivalists, saying to
their converts at the penitent form, in the language of the
day: 'Only believe, and God will set thee at liberty in a
moment.' Their antinomianism, if such it was, was more
apparent than real; at any rate, their fellow-reformers,
who held tenaciously to Wesley's teaching, were not
conscious that there was any difference of doctrine between
them. Perhaps the 'head and front of their offending' was

[19] *The Methodist Story* (London 1955), p. 87.

[20] G. J. Stevenson, *Methodist Worthies* (London 1886), VI.927.

[21] e.g. Townsend, Workman, and Eayrs, *New History of Methodism* (London 1909), I.427.

[22] ibid.

[23] W. Redfern, *Modern Developments in Methodism* (London 1906), p. 126.

rather that, like the other revivalists of the time, the Bible Christians and the Primitive Methodists, they employed women preachers, contrary to the general policy of the Wesleyan Conference.[24] The most famous of these was Elizabeth Evans, immortalized as 'Dinah Morris' in her niece George Eliot's *Adam Bede*—a tablet to her memory is placed in the Wirksworth Methodist (Free) Church,[25] where she used to worship. In addition to their headquarters in Derby, the Arminian Methodists had also societies or circuits at Leicester, Nottingham, and Redditch, and altogether brought into the Union some 1,200 members and seventy local preachers.

The years between 1837 and 1849 were years of growth and development; almost all the familiar features of Methodist Church life gradually emerged. A 'Home Mission and Connexional Fund' was started in 1837, as also were a Bookroom and a connexional magazine; a 'Thankoffering Fund' to celebrate the centenary of Methodism, to be devoted to various causes, was set up in 1839, and a Chapel Relief Fund and a Preachers' Annuitant Society in 1841. The year 1842 saw the establishment of the Preachers' Children's Fund, and 1843 a 'Beneficent Fund' for the temporary assistance of ministers suffering from personal or domestic affliction.

These years were of course the 'Hungry Forties', and the troubles and poverty of the time are reflected in the records of the Association. In 1842 the report on the 'General State of the Connexion' drew attention to a decrease in membership, and attributed it to the 'commercial distress existing most extensively in those parts of the kingdom where our Societies are most numerous; many of the members of the Society having absented themselves from their classes and from Public Worship in consequence of their extreme poverty and inability to

---

[24] cf. W. F. Swift, 'The Women Itinerant Preachers of Early Methodism' in *WHS Proc.*, XXVIII.89ff.

[25] So says Redfern, op. cit. p. 126; but the Superintendent of the Wirksworth Circuit informs the present writer that it is in Ebenezer ex-Wesleyan Chapel.

obtain decent clothing'.[26] In 1844 there was a decrease of over 5,500, rather more than one-fifth of the total membership, but it was largely due to the lack of numerical returns from Jamaica, which the previous year had reported 4,400 members. On the other hand, there was a serious deficiency in Connexional Funds, to remedy which, 'it is expected that each of the itinerant preachers advance the sum of £5; and that to reimburse themselves, they be allowed to solicit special contributions in their respective circuits'.[27] (Lest this should seem a strange procedure, it may be worth noting that when in 1849 the Wesleyan Children's Fund was embarrassed, a committee recommended that 'certain sums should be contributed by different classes of ministers to make up the deficiency'.)[28] In addition, the stipends of ministers in full connexion were reduced to £80, and those of probationers to £55, Home Missionaries being employed at even lower stipends. Three years later there was further embarrassment in the Connexional finances as a result of the general depression in trade, and the stipends of married Home Missionaries were reduced to £60. The same trouble the following year prevented additional men being called into the ranks of the Ministry.

But there was a brighter side; accessions of strength continued, both of members and of ministers. In 1838 Thomas Pennock, a Wesleyan minister in Jamaica, joined the Association with upwards of 3,000 of his members, thus constituting the first overseas missionary work of the Churches. At the same time, a Wesleyan probationer, Kelsham Fullager, seceded and was sent to reinforce the Jamaican staff. Furthermore, some 'Independent Wesleyan' circuits in North Wales asked to be accepted, and Aberystwyth, Bodedryn (near Holyhead), and Tryddyn appear at various times in the *Minutes*. News of reform had spread to the other side of the world, and the same

---

[26] *Minutes* (1842), p. 22.

[27] *Minutes* (1844), p. 21.

[28] Samuel Harrison, *A Companion to the Minutes* (London and Sheffield 1849), p. 121.

year the Van Dieman's Land Wesleyan Methodist Association applied to be recognized, the Methodist Protestant
Church at Halifax, Nova Scotia, made a similar application, and requests came for missionaries to be sent to
Carrickfergus and Hamburg. Was it, incidentally, the
application from Tasmania that made the Association
think of changing their name by the addition of the word
Methodist? For in 1839 it was decided, after a year's
consideration, to insert that word in the denomination's
designation,[29] though 'Wesleyan Methodist Association'
does not appear on the title page of the *Minutes* till the
following year. In 1839, too, it was reported that a score
of members and one local preacher had emigrated to
Australia and intended to keep up their connexion with
the Association. In 1841 Prince Edward Island was added
to the Stations, a Society in that place, with its Minister,
Matthew Smith, having asked for recognition. The same
year communications were opened with the Protestant
Methodists of America, but the question of a 'fraternal
union' was postponed until the Assembly was assured that
that Church did not in any way countenance slavery.[30]
Another minister, James B. Ambler, and Church, in St.
John's, New Brunswick, joined the Association in 1842,
and in 1845 a number of Associationist emigrants from
Cornwall to Wisconsin asked for a missionary to labour
among them; William Drummond was sent. In 1848 a
letter was read from the 'Wesleyan Methodist Connexion'
in America, consisting of 17,000 members and some 500
preachers 'stationed and unstationed', who had seceded
from the Methodist Episcopal Church on the question of
slavery; and fraternal relations with that body were
consequently opened.

Thus, by 1849, when the next and greatest upheaval in
Methodism took place, the small nucleus of the UMFC,
numbering some 21,500 members, had established themselves as a truly and distinctively Methodist Connexion,
and had a small but vigorous missionary enterprise, even
though one or two of the small secessions—such as that

[29] *Minutes* (1839), p. 10.   [30] ibid. (1841), pp. 27f.

of the circuit on Prince Edward Island—were not destined to last more than a year or so.

The last and numerically largest branch was of course the Wesleyan Reformers. The story has often been told (and a sad story it is), so that there is no need to go at great length into the details of the troubles that led to the exclusion of James Everett, Samuel Dunn and William Griffith in 1849. In 1846 Wesleyan ministers received by post an anonymous pamphlet: *Fly Sheets from the 'Private Correspondent', No.* 1, with the colophon: 'By order of the Corresponding Committee for detecting, exposing, and correcting abuses. London, Manchester, Bristol, Liverpool, Birmingham, Leeds, Hull, Glasgow, 1846.' A second was issued later the same year, a third in 1847, a fourth in 1848, and a fifth and last, shorter than the others, after the expulsions in 1849. Had no notice been taken of them, they would have been consigned to oblivion; had their charges been answered or disproved, good would have been done and their author or authors discredited. But they chiefly attacked Dr Bunting, the Mission House staff, and his friends (the whole regarded as the London clique), and Bunting with all his undoubted gifts—and it were idle to pretend that they were not many—was almost unbelievably touchy and childish where his personal reputation was concerned. He and his friends were therefore determined to seek out the anonymous authors, if more than one there were. Consequently Dr George Osborn was allowed to circulate a 'declaration' among the ministers of the Connexion: 'We, the undersigned, agree to declare that we regard with indignation and abhorrence the anonymous attacks on the motives and character of our Brethren that have recently appeared in certain clandestine publications; that we have never intentionally communicated with the authors of those publications, with a view to afford information and assistance . . .', etc.[31] By the close of the Conference, the 'test' had been signed by 650 brethren; copies were then sent to other preachers, some of whom signed and others held

[31] *Wesleyan Delegate Takings* (Manchester and London 1850), p. xi.

back; three months later, in October 1847, another copy was sent to those who had so far not signed, and a third copy a year later to those still declining. When Conference 1849 opened in Manchester, thirty-six signatures were still missing. This was too many to have had a hand in the *Fly Sheets*, and too many to expel. Consequently Dr Osborn in Conference sought to examine a few of them. His first victim was Joshua Fielden. Dr Joseph Beaumont, one of the leading 'liberals' in the Conference, interpolated that it was 'unworthy to begin with an aged man pressed down by infirmities'; but Dr Osborn would not let go until the old man had raised his right hand, trembling like an aspen leaf, and said: 'This hand for years has not been able to write.' James Everett was sent for from York and Dr Hannah, the Secretary of Conference, 'read, from a paper in his hand, the question: "Are you the writer or author of the *Fly Sheets*?"

'Mr Everett: "Am I the first on the list of those who have not signed the declaration? When the brethren whose names occur in the *Minutes* before mine have answered the question, then will I. Why am I singled out from the rest?"

'The Secretary, without answering, persistently pressed the question, till Mr Everett said: "I demand the name of my accuser, the charge against me in writing, and an opportunity to defend myself in a constitutional way."

'After further interlocutions with the Secretary, he positively refused to answer under any other conditions than those already mentioned, saying: "If I am the most suspected, then there must be the most evidence against me; produce it." '[32]

After deferring decision for a day or so, and giving the accused time to reconsider and talk the matter over with a deputation, Everett was finally expelled, though he had been forty-two years in the Ministry, and was one of its most distinguished writers. Later William Griffith and Samuel Dunn were called upon to answer the so-called 'friendly question' and because they refused to answer

[32] Gregory, *Sidelights on the Conflicts of Methodism*, p. 452.

incriminating questions put to them, and refused to promise to desist from sending communications to the *Wesleyan Times* and to discontinue the *Wesley Banner* (two 'liberal' periodicals), they were expelled.

'If I am the most suspected, then there must be the most evidence against me; produce it'—so said Everett. But no evidence *was* brought against him in support of his supposed authorship; and it never *has* been proved that he was the author. Richard Chew, in his able and authoritative 'Life',[33] says, 'Everett has never been proved to be the author, in whole or in part, of the *Fly Sheets*'; and goes on to say that the wording of the resolution on his expulsion—'the strong and generally prevalent suspicion'—shows the impossibility the Conference found in proving his authorship; they would not have used the word 'suspicion' if 'proof' could have been used. On the other hand, Everett had a known predilection for anonymity—witness his greatest work, *Methodism as it is*, published anonymously; his *Wesleyan Centenary Takings*, likewise anonymous, and attributed to himself in his *Methodism as it is*;[34] and his *Gatherings from the Pit Heaps* by 'Coleman Collier'. Furthermore, the long preface to the *Centenary Takings* contains outspoken reflections on Bunting and on Mission House extravagance—the favourite theme of the *Fly Sheets*. Finally one quotation, and its parallel in a letter of Everett's, may be of interest—in number 5 appear the words: 'Our reader may expect some revelations on this subject, which will be more annoying to the officers than on a certain occasion the "ringing of the bells" was to Samuel Jackson, as Governor of Richmond Branch.'[35] Now in an autograph letter in the writer's possession, written by Everett to an unnamed correspondent on 30th March 1849, we read: 'The conduct of the Governor of Richmond astonishes me. . . . The ringing a few chimes to the good man was an exercise worthy of the lads.' It is

---

[33] *James Everett, a Biography* (London 1875), p. 399.
[34] See quotation in *UMFC Magazine* (1864), where the story of the origin of the *Takings* is told, pp. 516ff.
[35] *A Faithful Verbatim Reprint of the Fly Sheets* . . . (Birmingham, n.d.), p. 122.

when small and unimportant details correspond that the suspicion of identical authorship is strongest. By a strange coincidence, another phrase in the same letter, ' "Doth Job serve God for naught?" No, nor Jabez neither', is re-echoed in the first *Fly Sheet* and applied to the same person, Dr Bunting. In spite of the defence of Everett by his admirers of last century, all of whom insist that his authorship was never proved, the present writer feels that it cannot be denied.

But why should the *Fly Sheets* have been anonymous at all? For answer, let Everett speak for himself: 'There is wisdom in working under cover, when it is certain you would not be listened to openly. Under cover we can go unmolested, till the whole tale is told—till the whole case is opened; otherwise, an endeavour would be made to stop us at the outset.'[36] Had the writer divulged his name (or names, if there were more than one), connexional extermination would have been swift and sure. For Everett was not a coward, not ashamed of his opinions. 'Had there been a fair field, where facts and arguments without favour or prejudice could wrestle with each other, concealment would have been cowardly and dishonourable.'[37] But it must be admitted—and Gregory, so warm an admirer of Bunting's greatness, makes no attempt to belittle the fact—that there was *not* a fair field; those who attacked Bunting, or indeed any isolated policy of his, could count on the displeasure of the bulk of Conference, while those who supported him and the official circle could use what measures they chose. When that happens, honest men are driven to excess; it is that which makes revolutionaries. Many words were applied to the *Fly Sheets* because they were anonymous; but the Book Room published, advertised, and sold the *Papers on Wesleyan Matters*, also anonymous, which contained attacks on Joseph Fowler, the Secretary of the Conference, which William Maclardie Bunting, the saintly son of the 'Dictator', pronounced 'to be worse than anything in the *Fly*

[36] Quoted in W. Redfern, *Modern Developments in Methodism*, p. 131.
[37] R. Chew, op. cit. p. 378.

C

Sheets'. Critical papers, such as the *Wesleyan Times* and the *Wesley Banner*, were loaded with abuse, but the *Watchman* was constantly favoured and protected from criticism, even though it 'too successfully endeavoured to out-Everett Everett in vituperation and abuse',[38] and on occasion 'exceeded far in coarseness and vulgarity anything which had discoloured the *Fly Sheets*. This certainly deserved the epithets applied to the *Fly Sheets*—"slimy and disreputable".'[39]

What could, it may be asked at this point of time, for there has arisen a generation which knew not Jabez, what could have caused all this controversy? Turn to the titles of the *Fly Sheets*. The first dealt with 'Location, Centralization, and Secularization'—officials stayed too long in office, and were all, or nearly all, located too long in London; hence they were suspected of cliquism and secret intrigues. Connexional committees were the preserve of a select few. The second number dealt with 'The Presidential Chair, the Platform, and the Connexional Committee'; the mode of electing the latter should be changed. The fourth dealt with the Stationing Committee, which it stigmatized as 'the slaughter-house of ministerial character'. On almost every page, Dr Bunting's name appears in an unfavourable light. The question that naturally strikes one is: Were these charges true? William Redfern, writing soberly in 1906 says, 'Substantially, though perhaps not in every particular, the statements were true'[40]—which no doubt is why they were never answered, and why, instead, attention was drawn to discovering if possible the anonymous author.

Something must be said of Jabez Bunting. Dr John Kent has described him as the 'last Wesleyan'—he was perhaps the greatest Methodist since Wesley (Adam Clarke might be the only other aspirant to that title). Gregory speaks of his 'surpassing genius for organization and administration', and notes that he was 'a mighty theologian', 'a born orator, a born financier, a born debater, a born pleader'. 'All acquit him of selfishness;

[38] Gregory, op. cit. p. 436.   [39] ibid.   [40] op. cit. p. 130.

all unite in giving him credit for the purest motives; and
when his proceedings are viewed in the aggregate, he will
be found to be generally philanthropic in his views,
feelings, and purposes. But we again enquire—How has he
obtained such ascendancy in the body? Not by fraud,
not by misconduct; but by lending his superior talents to
promote the best interests of the Connexion.' And those
words, strange as it may seem, were written by Everett in
an anonymous work which aroused Bunting's wrath.[41]
They are only equalled by the warm tribute to him in
Recollections of Methodism at Leeds, where we read: 'His
knowledge of the human heart, its depravity, and the
means for its recovery, was profound; his statements of
divine truth were singularly clear and cogent; his reason-
ings forcible and satisfactory; whilst his appeals to the
judgement and conscience were such as I may, without
hesitation, say, I never heard equalled by any other
preacher of the Gospel. . . . But there was one other important qualification as a minister of the Gospel in which Mr
Bunting greatly excelled, and that was an extraordinary
gift of prayer. Such earnest, heartfelt pleadings with the
Almighty were seldom heard in the pulpit, or from the
lips of any other man. . . .'[42] That, and much more in
the same strain, was the testimony of Matthew Johnson,
one of the men expelled in 1827 as a result of Bunting's
intervention in the Leeds Organ Case.

But he was, to use his son's word, 'masterful', and could
not brook opposition. Like a spoilt child, if he could not
have his own way, he 'would not play'. On one occasion,
when crossed, he threatened to leave the Presidential
Chair and dissolve Conference; on another, for a similar
reason, he threatened to resign all his offices. The story is
told that Charles Wesley threatened once to leave the
room when his point was not carried, and John replied:
'Reach my brother his hat.' It might have been better if
Conference had once or twice reached Bunting his hat!

[41] *Wesleyan Takings*, 3rd ed. (London 1841), I.11. There is much more
in the same strain.
[42] *Magazine* (1863), p. 150.

But instead, Conference fawned, and grew hysterical. This sort of thing constantly occurred: 'The Doctor, who was repeatedly and vociferously cheered, sat down amidst applause, much prolonged and more than once renewed'[43] —and that after an emotional defence of himself by Dr Bunting. The reading of a letter from James Bromley (one of the 'opposition') 'produced from time to time vociferous expressions of disapprobation and abhorrence'.[44]

Such was the temper of Conference and its leading officials; similar examples could be quoted a hundredfold. Such was the unjudicial atmosphere in which minorities and dissentients tried in vain for a fair hearing. It was grossly unfair to men with an honest but independent conviction, and did them grave personal harm. It was no doubt, in part, the memory of the high-handedness of Conference, and particularly of Bunting, that kindled that positive passion for the rights of minorities and for an impartial chair that characterized the best and most typical members of the UMFC.

The expulsion of the three men staggered the nation. That is no exaggeration. Even *The Times* remarked: 'Talk of the Star Chamber! A man might hold his tongue in that Court, take his trial, and escape if the evidence did not support the charge.'[45] A fortnight after the expulsions, an enormous meeting was held in Exeter Hall, which was the forerunner of crowded meetings the whole length and breadth of the country. During the year 'the three' attended some hundred and forty meetings, always crowded, attended in all by some 170,000 people. The following March an aggregate meeting of delegates met in the Albion Street Independent Chapel, London Wall, which passed a series of resolutions—mild enough in their demands—asking for reform in Methodism: for the right to hold meetings to discuss connexional affairs, for the representation of 'the people' in the Courts of the Church, for the leaders' meeting to have effective control of discipline, for the right of a meeting to continue even if the

---

[43] Harrison, *A Companion to the Minutes*, p. 72.   [44] ibid. p. 92.
[45] Quoted in Redfern, *Modern Developments in Methodism*, p. 134.

minister vacated the chair, and so on. It was felt that if these demands were conceded by Conference, trouble could be avoided, and peace restored. Year after year the delegates refused to organize as a separate community, hoping against hope that Conference would consent to meet them and make peace, and year after year they were unceremoniously repulsed.

Meanwhile expulsions and secessions were going on. It is not too much to say that, under many a superintendent who modelled himself on Bunting—who put into practice Bunting's doctrine of pastoral supremacy—any shadow of sympathy with reform was met by instant expulsion. The reformer might be advanced in years, a distinguished local citizen, a life-long servant of the Church, a beloved class leader or local preacher—it mattered nothing. In the list of delegates to the Albion Street meeting, thirty are noted as having been members of society over forty years —some over fifty. And when a leader was expelled, his whole class often followed him. Some whole societies were lost, others were bitterly split, and families were divided. Superintendents whose administration was mild were censured by the 1850 Conference for their mildness! In five years the parent Church lost 100,000 members, many of whom were lost to Methodism—even to the Christian Church—altogether.[46] Two examples must suffice, one of expulsion, one of its results. In Wakefield, G. W. Harrison, the first mayor of the town, was expelled for having lessened his subscription to the West Parade Chapel. In Arnold, near Nottingham, 'nearly two-thirds of the society went over to the Reformers, taking with them some of the musical instruments used in the chapel. One night a Reformer was returning from a meeting with

---

[46] It is perhaps an exaggeration to say that 'the majority were lost both to Methodism and to the Church as a whole' (Cyril Davey, *The Methodist Story*, p. 56), or 'only a few settled down in any other Christian community' (i.e. than the Mother Church; Frank Baker, *A Charge to Keep* (London 1947), p. 52). The Wesleyan Reformers reported their membership in 1852 as 47,598 with 1,547 on trial, but only 19,113 amalgamated in 1857; others did so later (cf. p. 47). Others joined the MNC. It would be extremely difficult to assess how many joined other denominations.

one of the disputed instruments in his possession, when he was waylaid by three "singers" in the Conference chapel. With some violence they wrested the instrument from his possession and left him lying in the roadway. All attempts to settle the dispute having failed, the three Conference chapel "singers" appeared before the magistrates and were fined 16s. 6d. each including costs.'[47] Such stories were multiplied up and down the country; for the whole of the country experienced revulsion. The Reformers in 1850 had their sympathizers in places as far apart as Cardiff, Carlisle, Dover, Newcastle, Exeter, and Swansea; by 1852 delegates attended the annual meeting from Cornwall and Scotland. In some places, where virtually the whole of the society seceded, they were successful in taking their chapel with them, and more than one UMFC chapel had the words 'Wesleyan Chapel' over its door to the end of its days; in other places, members had to leave dearly loved sanctuaries, built by their self-sacrifice and labour, to worship in warehouses. An immense personal and practical loyalty to 'the three expelled' manifested itself; funds were raised for the three men, totalling between three and four thousand pounds, and later other sums for James Bromley, expelled the following year.

It was at the delegate meeting of 1852 in Sheffield (Conference met there at the same time) that the first step was taken by the Reformers toward independence and establishment as a denomination, though for a long time yet they hoped for a reconciliation with Conference and declined to regard themselves as other than Wesleyan Methodists—witness their class tickets which were headed 'Wesleyan Methodist Society. Established 1739' as late as June 1865. But in 1852 they drew up their 'Declaration of Principles' which, in a word, proclaimed the internal independence of all local courts, the right of free discussion on any matters affecting the interest of the Church, the right of all Church members to take part in all Church

---

[47] Rowland C. Swift, 'The Wesleyan Reform Movement in Nottingham', in *WHS Proc.*, XXVIII.79.

business meetings, and lastly, 'That preachers of the Gospel are not "Lords over God's heritage", for "One is your Master, even Christ, and all ye are Brethren" '.[48] With those principles, all the preceding secessions would agree.

[48] Quoted in W. H. Jones, *History of the Wesleyan Reform Union* (London 1952), p. 39.

II

UNITED

From their earliest days, the first of the secessionists looked forward to Union with other branches of the Methodist family. We have already seen how Protestant Methodists, Arminian Methodists, and others, joined the Wesleyan Methodist Association. But that was not enough. The earliest Assembly—that of the Wesleyan Association in 1836—resolved 'that the meeting is deeply impressed with the conviction of the desirableness of a union—on New Testament principles—of all the branches of the Methodist Family, and it is an instruction to the Committee . . . to take into their most serious consideration, and report to the Meeting, what measures can be adopted to effect such a purpose, at the earliest practicable period';[1] and that resolution is amplified in succeeding minutes of the same year's Assembly. Similar words are recorded the following year, when the Connexional Committee reported a contemplated union with the Methodist New Connexion. Negotiations broke down, however, because the Associationists were not prepared to allow 'legislative authority' to the Conference, and because it was evident that the New Connexion was not prepared to consider any alteration of its own constitution. Such a union would not be union, but absorption. In 1844 Robert Eckett, then Secretary of the Annual Assembly, proposed to the New Connexion the establishment of a Federal Council of Dissenting Methodists, with some such title as 'The Wesleyan Dissenting Union, for the Advancement of Religious Freedom'. It was a private move of Eckett's, which he similarly addressed to the Primitive Methodists and to the Bible Christians; but the Assembly confirmed Eckett's action,[2] and the New Connexion Conference

[1] *Minutes* (1836), p. 11.   [2] ibid. (1844), p. 29.

replied rather vaguely in 1846, praying 'that the various sections of Methodism may, in the true spirit of Christianity, be brought more closely together', and that 'the best spirit of brotherly kindness and unanimity may pervade all our denominations'.[3] The Assembly replied, in effect, that they were not talking about a 'spirit of brotherly kindness', but about 'union with all the branches of the Methodist family'.[4] Passages in the Jubilee Volume of the New Connexion reflecting on the Association, and Robert Eckett's pamphlets in reply, did away with any hope of a *rapprochement* along those lines for some years to come;[5] Eckett was thanked by the Annual Assembly.[6]

Relationships with the Wesleyan Reformers were opened, almost inauspiciously, in 1851. The proceedings of the 1849 Wesleyan Conference had clearly exercised the minds of many Methodists other than Wesleyans, and a number of memorials on the validity of 'question by penalty' were sent to the Assembly. That body replied by deprecating the excitement, and pointing out that such procedure could not take place in the Association Assembly. But in the same Assembly an 'Address' from the Wesleyan Reformers was read (an Address to all the 'Protestant Evangelical Churches'), to which a reply was sent, pointing out that both Reformers and Association had arisen from similar causes, and that for that reason the Assembly was gratified to find 'that large accessions have been made to the number of Methodists who acknowledge the Scriptural right of churches to self government',[7] and that it looked forward to the day of Methodist union, 'having a Church polity entirely accordant with the teachings of our Lord Jesus Christ and His holy apostles'.[8]

In 1853 and 1854 the resolution of the 1836 Assembly (repeated in 1837) was reiterated and 'given teeth', so to speak, by authorizing the Connexional Committee to conduct negotiations with any branches of Methodism who were prepared to discuss amalgamation: 'This Assembly

---

[3] *Minutes* (1846), p. 32. [4] ibid.
[5] *The Jubilee of the Methodist New Connexion* (London 1848), pp. 354, 383.
[6] *Minutes* (1849), p. 34. [7] ibid. (1851), p. 33. [8] ibid.

will also rejoice if a closer union can be effected, on Scriptural principles, between all or any of the sections of the Methodist family; and therefore authorizes the Connexional Committee to take such action as it may deem advisable, in furtherance of the purposes referred to in this resolution.'[9] At the same time, the Reform delegates were meeting in Birmingham, where Mr Hildreth Kay of London, one of the leading laymen among the Reformers, moved that communications be opened 'with the various branches of the Wesleyan family';[10] he was appointed secretary of the committee to conduct the correspondence, and so wrote to each branch of Methodism. The New Connexion was apparently only prepared to consider union on the basis of its own constitution; but when the Connexional Committee of the Association received the communication at their meeting in Winsford, Cheshire, on 1st November 1854,[11] they appointed twelve representatives—six ministers and six laymen—to meet a similar number of Reform representatives. This united committee met in Nottingham on 27th February 1855. The Reform representatives presented a paper outlining a declaration of their principles, and these were discussed with the utmost candour; so that when the Committee met again in June in Rochdale, 'A draft basis of union was agreed upon with almost perfect unanimity'.[12] This basis of union was forwarded to all the circuits of the Association—and not one circuit objected to its adoption by the Association. The terms were approved by the 1855 Assembly, who suggested a joint Assembly in 1856; the Reformers at their delegate meeting, gathered at the same time as the Assembly, proposed one or two slight emendations, together with the proviso that the union should only be consummated if two-thirds of the Reformers were in agreement. The two meetings kept each other informed of suggested modifications in the proposed

[9] *Minutes* (1853), p. 39.
[10] *Wesleyan Methodist Penny Magazine* (1854), p. 140.
[11] *Magazine* (1854), p. 571.
[12] W. J. Townsend, *Story of Methodist Union* (London, n.d., c. 1906), p. 90.

basis of union by telegraph; and a writer in the connexional *Magazine* writes, in typical mid-Victorian phrase-
ology, that 'we will venture to affirm, that never was this
subtle machinery for the transmission of thought more
worthily employed than in this instance'!

The Reformers' proviso meant that the union was put
back a year; the requisite two-thirds approval could not
be obtained in time. But in 1856 final points were agreed
on, and, provided the two-thirds concurrence to the final
terms could be obtained in the Reform Delegate Meeting,
the joint committee, now increased to twenty-one on
each side, was empowered to complete the union and
determine how it should be celebrated. Consequently that
year the Assembly was adjourned (rather than dissolved)
to such a place as the joint committee should determine.
On 14th May 1857 this committee met at Exeter Hall,
London, and resolved:

That subject to the basis of union and the other arrangements
that have been mutually adopted by the special committee of
the Methodist Reformers and of the Wesleyan Methodist
Association, the said committees mutually declare that the
proposed amalgamation of the churches represented by the
said committees has now been effected.[13]

It is of course well known that the whole of the Reformers did not enter that amalgamation; it had been
specifically stated that, in conformity with the measure of
independence each local church enjoyed, any church
was at liberty to remain outside the union, just as any
church was at liberty to become reunited to the 'Conference Connexion'[14] when it had a liberal government.[15]
And the present Wesleyan Reform Union is of course the
successor to those who chose to remain independent in
1857 and succeeding years. But even before the union of

13 Townsend, ibid. p. 91.

14 This designation perhaps explains the use of the word 'Assembly' for
the annual meeting of the Association and later of the UMFC. 'Conference
Methodists' was another way of saying 'Wesleyan Methodists'; but was
preferred as the dissenters always claimed to be true *Wesleyan* Methodists.

15 *Minutes* (1853), p. 39.

1857 some Reformers had joined. The Bath Association Circuit in 1856 reported an accession from their ranks, and the same year's report on the 'Spiritual and Numerical State of the Connexion' noted that there were 'several Reform Societies, which have been for some months virtually united with the Association'.[16]

The 1857 Assembly of the Wesleyan Methodist Association, together with such Wesleyan Reform circuits as had united, met in the historic Baillie Street Chapel, Rochdale. This sanctuary, the citadel *par excellence* of Free Methodism, was built as an Association chapel in 1836 and was the scene of no fewer than five Association Assemblies before the Uniting Assembly of 1857; thenceforward, it was the scene of four UMFC Assemblies and two United Methodist Conferences. No fewer than fourteen of its ministers have been President of one or other of the Assemblies, four of them serving twice; and Sir James Duckworth, one of Baillie Street's leading laymen, was one of the two laymen elected to the Presidency of the UMFC. Furthermore, in the first century of its history, there was never a year when there was not at least one Baillie Street man on the Town Council, and fifteen mayors came from the chapel, many of them serving more than one year. One wonders if any other church in Methodism has such a record.

To this chapel, then, the representatives of the amalgamating bodies came on 29th July 1857. Who was to be the first President? It would be strange if there were not a little apprehension and even jealousy, especially on the part of the Reformers; for the Association had a slight advantage in membership (the *Minutes* report 20,873 Association members and 19,113 Reformers),[17] but considerably more representatives. The leading men of either tradition were nominated, James Everett and Robert Eckett. But when the vote was taken the Reformer Everett had sixty-eight votes to Eckett's twenty-eight;

[16] *Minutes* (1856), p. 19.
[17] Some 35,000 had voted for the Union; cf. *Wesleyan Methodist Penny Magazine* (1857), p. 210.

one was cast for James Molineux. That augured well
for the future, and must have been immensely reassuring
to the smaller body. Indeed, in those early days, a
marked courtesy toward each other—'in honour pre-
ferring one another'—is most noticeable. And the result
of the voting for the Presidency led to Eckett's being
elected Secretary with ninety-five votes, compared with
one for each of three other men. There were no guarantees to ensure that each party received its fair share of
appointments, any more than there were guarantees that
ministers and laymen should be equally represented. But
in 1858, when the voting came to be counted for the
Connexional Committee, it was found that out of fifty-nine
names put forward, the twenty elected comprised ten
ministers and ten laymen, ten Reformers and ten Associationists. No wonder they boasted of their 'free election'
when the results were such as these!

One of the most important matters to be discussed at
that first Assembly was naturally the future designation
of the denomination. Eckett reported a number of names
that had been suggested, such as 'Wesleyan Free Church'
and 'Methodist Reform Church'. It was necessary to
choose a term that would stand for the whole, but which
would allow local liberty; consequently he proposed 'The
United Methodist Churches', which would allow other
churches and circuits to amalgamate without changing
their own name. It transpired that that name was favoured by the Associationists, whereas the Reformers preferred 'Wesleyan Methodist Free Church'. During a long
debate, other suggestions came, not unnaturally, from the
floor: 'Methodist Free Churches', 'Methodist Reform
Churches', and 'Methodist Congregational Churches' all
had their protagonists. Then Mr John Benson, a Reformer
from Newcastle-on-Tyne, who had been elected one of the
Assistant Secretaries, suggested 'United Methodist Free
Churches', interpolating the word 'Free' in order to
encourage other Reformers to join. John Wesley Gilchrist
of Camelford protested that there were congregations
calling themselves 'Free Methodists' in Camborne and

St Austell who would not be likely to unite, hence 'United Methodist Free Churches' would be misleading and inconvenient. The representatives from Northwich reported that their circuit preferred 'Methodist Free Church'; and in the course of the debate, Joseph Chipchase, a leading lay Reformer from London, remarked: 'They were about the only section of the Methodist body who could lay claim to be wholly and entirely [free]'. In defence of the plural form 'Churches', Eckett urged that 'They would be the only body which consisted of united churches. . . . The Methodist Conference constituted only one church, and so with the others.' (It is interesting to note that the other Methodist bodies had not yet adopted the word 'Church' as part of their title.)

Finally, as an amendment to Eckett's proposition, the insertion of the word 'Free' was formally proposed, and the amendment carried by seventy-two votes to thirty-three for the original motion. The debate was then adjourned to see if a formula acceptable to all could be found; but on the resumption, Eckett proposed to insert the word 'Free', as in the amendment, and asked for the approval of three-quarters of the Assembly, in order to comply with the provisions of the Foundation Deed of the Association (which required the consent of three-quarters of the members of two successive Assemblies). Consequently the name 'United Methodist Free Churches' was almost unanimously adopted, and the decision celebrated by the singing of the Doxology. The new designation was unanimously confirmed the following year; and in the course of the business, John Benson made a remark that is still very much to the point: 'The word "Church" ', he said, 'was often used to designate the bricks and mortar of the house in which men met to worship, and he hoped that they, as Dissenters, who professed to believe that the term was applicable strictly to the corporate body of believers, would not use it to designate a mere building.'

Rather unwisely, the Assembly decided to anticipate this confirmation. The new name was put on the first class-ticket in September 1857, and the title-page of the

1857 *Minutes* contains the same words. The authorities were clearly in two minds on the matter, for although the *Minutes* were 'Signed on behalf of the Annual Assembly of the United Churches of the Wesleyan Methodist Association and Methodist Reformers',[18] the annual addresses were 'To the United Methodist Free Churches'. It was no doubt a practical difficulty which led to the anticipation on the tickets. But to anticipate confirmation is always unwise; it gives the impression of prejudging the issue and forcing the hands of those who have to decide. Little wonder, then, that the writers in the *Wesleyan Methodist Penny Magazine* for 1857, the organ of the Wesleyan Reform Committee, while not merely friendly to, but positively encouraging, amalgamation, pointed out with sadness that the tickets' wording had been 'rushed'—'a most crude and ill-digested affair'.[19] As may be imagined, too, exception was taken to the issue, automatically, of the *Minutes* from the old Association Book Room. The non-amalgamating Reformers rather tended to regard the Associationists as expecting always to have the last word; and complained that the Reform representatives had been too often asleep! Perhaps the trouble was that the Secretary, Robert Eckett, was too eloquent![20] In short, the Reformers were, rather naturally, a little wary lest any of the principles for which they had striven and suffered expulsion should be thrown away.

But in the newly-formed Connexion there were no such qualms. Over the next few years, circuits and individual churches continued to amalgamate,[21] so that the joint membership which in 1857 was 39,968 had reached 67,488 ten years later, with over 6,000 on trial. The reason for this was simple: 'There was no concession on either side; on all leading principles there was perfect

[18] *Minutes* (1857), p. 56.

[19] op. cit. p. 166.

[20] ibid. p. 132. They noted, with apprehension, that Eckett had been Secretary for a number of years.

[21] For example, the 1869 *Minutes* (p. 79) report that WR Churches (possibly 'circuits' is meant in some cases) at Yeadon, Elland, Driffield, and Aberdeen had amalgamated during the year.

identity of view. To describe the basis of union in the briefest manner, it was an attempt to construct a system which would unite Connexionalism and Congregationalism, the cohesion of the one with the freedom of the other. It gave to the Annual Conference or Assembly the least amount of power compatible with the public good, and to the circuits or churches the utmost freedom consistent with Connexional unity.'[22] The *Watchman*, the Conference journal that had caused so much trouble in 1849, might be sarcastic: 'There is to be tried a new thing, which has no name as yet, and is neither Independency nor Connexionalism. . . . Either the constitution will change, or the body will die, and its component parts be dissipated hither and thither.'[23] But it was not new, for it had been the polity of the Association for twenty years; and the new Connexion did not die, but grew both by normal accession and by the amalgamation of other Reformers. 'Much more than might have been anticipated, the ex-Associationists and ex-Reformers have forgotten their previous distinctions, and acted as members of one community for the prosperity of which all should be equally concerned.'[24] It was soon impossible to tell who was of one tradition and who of the other.

Not that everything was plain sailing. There were tricky problems to solve, not the least being that concerning the ex-Reform ministers; for it was open to any circuit to do without a minister, and there were more Reform ministers who came into the Union than there were circuits taking a minister; which could have meant more ministers than the United Churches could station. But that problem and others always incidental to amalgamation were solved. And increasingly, in spite of the theoretically loose bond that joined them—they were described as a 'rope of sand', and boasted of their local independence—they had a real connexional loyalty that was rarely in question.

[22] J. Kirsop, *Historic Sketches of Free Methodism* (London 1885), p. 47.
[23] ibid.
[24] *Magazine* (1862), p. 606; the whole of this article is instructive.

III

METHODIST

It has often been noted that one of the great cementing forces which made possible the Union of 1932—and, to a lesser extent, the earlier unions—was the fact that in doctrine the various branches of Methodism were one, one too in that they all contained the distinguishing features that they had known from birth in parent Methodism; they prized

> *. . . her heavenly ways,*
> *Her sweet communion, solemn vows,*
> *Her hymns of love and praise.*

Apart from matters of administration, the branches of Methodism were always one. They all had an annual conference (even if the UMFC, or 'Free Methodists', as they generally called themselves for simplicity's sake, did call it an 'Annual Assembly', so many memories had the word 'Conference' for them), with a President elected annually. They were all arranged in circuits, and they all, even the Free Methodists, set up District Meetings, though their duties were severely circumscribed. They all rejoiced in their common Methodist ancestry—witness the first *Minutes* of the Wesleyan Association in 1836 when, in their 'General Principles', they declare, 'That on subjects of Doctrine, they entertain views according with those which were generally taught by Mr Wesley, and are admitted by the various branches of the Methodist community as consistent with the Holy Scriptures';[1] and witness also the similar declarations which were often made by speakers at stone-laying ceremonies. This loyalty to Methodist doctrine is perhaps best illustrated by

---

[1] *Minutes* (1836), p. 11.

the hymn-book. No doubt the first seceders (if that is the right word, for they were more often thrust out than stirred to secede) used the Methodist hymn-book of the day; but the Wesleyan Reform delegates meeting in Sheffield in 1852 spoke of the 'untradesman-like' business methods of the Wesleyan Book Room, and determined to publish their own hymn-book to avoid the necessity of obtaining copies from City Road. Consequently James Everett was asked to compile a new book. When it appeared in 1853, the 'Advertisement' stated that 'the only variation between this edition and that in general use, will be found in what has hitherto been termed the "Supplement".' They called it the *Wesleyan Methodist Hymn-book*, and continued to do so even as late as 1864. They further stressed their loyalty to essential Wesleyanism by prefacing the author's name to each hymn, and by printing the portrait of Wesley facing the title page—as the contemporary Wesleyan books did. Thus the Reformers proclaimed that they had no quarrel with Wesley or his teaching, but only with that of some of his followers. In 1859, the Annual Assembly, again meeting in Sheffield, determined to issue a new book; but again the current Wesleyan hymn-book was to be copied, apart from the Supplement, and again Wesley's portrait was prefixed to the book and Wesley's famous preface inserted after the new preface. Books printed at least as late as 1878 bore the portrait. A completely new book was issued in 1889, in which many nineteenth-century hymn-writers were represented, and only a third of the hymns were by the Wesleys;[2] they ranked their contemporaries too high, as most of us do!

We have seen that class-tickets, too, were a common feature. The Protestant Methodists used them, as did also the Association. From 1849 the Reformers printed a ticket similar in all respects to the current Wesleyan ticket (save that they could not anticipate the Wesleyan text, and the serial letter, in smaller type, was different),

[2] This compares with half by the Wesleys in the 1904 *Methodist Hymn-book*, and a quarter in our present book.

in pursuance of their policy and watchword, 'No secession'; and they were concerned at the appearance of the first UMFC ticket, because that issue did in fact signify secession.[3] Whoever chose the text among the other branches of Methodism (does not the Connexional Editor do so today?), with the UMFC the texts were generally chosen by the President.[4] Classes, as in parent Methodism, were the order of the day; and when the 1855-7 negotiations were taking place, the Reformers specially asked for a proposition to be inserted in the Deed of Union, which stated that '. . . as the Methodist Societies, for upwards of one hundred years, have proved the great value of weekly meetings in classes, . . . all who join us in church-fellowship are expected to meet in some one of the classes connected with the church'.[5] Bands, too, were still known; witness the note in the Rules of the Leeds Lady Lane Circuit: 'Band meetings, fellowship meetings . . . are recognised among us as means of grace, and have been found very useful'.[6]

As with the rest of Methodism, the annual *Minutes* of the Assembly were published, giving the resolutions of the Assembly, Stations of ministers, and, later on, the alphabetical list of names and addresses. Fuller records of church life are found in the magazines which each branch published. These have been classified in Dr Frank Cumbers's fascinating volume, *The Book Room*,[7] so there is no need to give details here. But it is worthwhile to say something of the *Large Magazine*, as they often called the magazine *par excellence*. In most respects it was similar to the other standard magazines of Methodism, containing articles on literature and divinity, sermons, obituaries, a considerable proportion of 'Religious Intelligence', and so on. Portraits appeared too; but the Book Room was presumably not

---

[3] *Wesleyan Methodist Penny Magazine* (1857), p. 133.

[4] *Magazine* (1859), p. 475.   [5] *Minutes* (1855), p. 42.

[6] 'Rules for the Government of the United Methodist Free Churches in the Leeds Lady Lane Circuit. 1866', p. 14.

[7] London 1956, pp. 148-9.

wealthy enough to afford one every month. There were normally three or four in the course of the year, and as one would expect of this Church, laymen as well as ministers appeared in the portrait gallery; on occasion, too, the print of a new chapel took the place of a portrait. The magazine of the Free Methodists was more distinctive in that with 1861 each month's magazine concluded with a 'Brief General Survey'. This feature was largely concerned with the progress of evangelical Christianity abroad and the relationship of political events to the spread of the Faith; but other subjects—not even excluding notorious murders!—were touched on from time to time. What really distinguished the *Free Methodist Magazine* was its treatment of the Annual Assembly. The other magazines of Methodism might publish the 'Stations' in the issue following Conference; they might also publish what we now call a 'digest' of what Conference did. But was it not the complaint of the Reformers that *the* Conference sat with closed doors, that the ordinary loyal member could know nothing of what transpired in that holy conclave, in that 'venerable assembly', as Conference was frequently described when the 'three expelled' defied it?[8] 'What have honest men to fear?' the Free Methodists were in the habit of declaiming. Consequently, their Assemblies from the very first were open not only to the Methodist public,[9] but also to the Press.[10] And that the wider Methodist public might know the course of debate, from the time of the Amalgamation onward the Assembly debates were reported at length in the *Magazine*, much after the style of today's *Methodist Recorder* reports of Conference; the report for 1861, for instance, runs to thirty-four pages. That style of magazine gave place to the lighter *Methodist Monthly* in 1892, with its many illustrations, fiction, and so on; among the casualties were the Conference reports.

As might be expected among a community who were brought to the birth and nurtured as a result of opposition

[8] cf. for instance, S. Harrison, *A Companion to the Minutes*, pp. 100, 110.
[9] *Minutes* (1836), p. 6.   [10] cf. e.g. *Minutes* (1857), p. 8.

to Bunting's doctrine of 'pastoral supremacy',[11] they were very suspicious of anything tending to enhance the 'status' of ministers. Methodism had long been accustomed to hearing the personal testimonies of the young men who were to be received into Full Connexion, and that was the order of the day with the Free Methodists. But whereas for some little time the 'Conference Methodists' had, as now, ordained during one of the sessions of Conference by the imposition of hands, that formality was anathema to the Free Methodists. The Reception Service to Full Connexion took place in an evening in the presence, and with the assistance, of the public; for after the candidates' testimonies, and the examination as to their call to the Ministry and belief in the doctrines and discipline of the Free Churches, each candidate's acceptance was then spontaneously moved and seconded by members of the Assembly, and carried by the vote of all present, including the general public. In a manifest sense, it was the act of the whole Church; they were 'publicly recognized', not only in the presence of, but by the will of, the Methodist public. The ordination hymn, 'The Saviour, when to heaven He rose', which now opens our Ordination Service, was often sung,[12] just as the Assembly was normally opened with the Methodist 'And are we yet alive?'

One by one, many of them in the early days, the various Methodist departments and funds were established. Both the sections that came together in 1857 had their own magazines and book rooms; and by that date the following

[11] The UMFC reflexion on Buntingism after thirty years is illustrated in the wording of the Address presented to William Griffith by the Beckett Street, Derby, congregation in 1879: 'Thirty years ago you were very reluctantly compelled, by a high conception of duty, to resist . . . and in conjunction with your noble Colleagues to wage a severe and unflinching conflict against, abuses of power and prerogative and arrogant pretensions on the part of some Wesleyan Ministers, utterly out of harmony and at variance with the spirit of Christ's teaching, the usages of the Primitive Church, and subversive of Christian freedom. This conflict . . . has won a great moral victory in the Founding of the United Methodist Free Churches on a liberal and Scriptural basis. . . .'

[12] e.g. *Magazine* (1862), p. 572.

funds and departments had become part of the normal life of the Association, and were taken over into the United Church: Chapel Relief Fund (established 1841), Preachers' Annuitant Society (1841), Preachers' Children's Fund (1842), Beneficent Fund 'for the temporary assistance of ministers suffering from personal or domestic affliction' (1843), Committee of Privileges 'to watch over the interests of the Connexion in reference to legislative enactments' (1843), and Sunday-school and Local Preachers' Fund (1846). Thereafter, a Foreign Missionary Committee was first established in 1860, Home and Foreign Mission Funds having been part of the general Connexional Funds until then. In 1862 the Annuitant Society and the Beneficent Fund were dissolved, and a new 'Preachers' Superannuation and Beneficent Fund' established, to enable the amalgamating Reform ministers to join; the previous Annuitant Society's funds had been almost entirely contributed by the Association ministers. A Home Missions scheme was set up in 1863, and the functions of District Meetings, which had first been rather tentatively set up in 1857 at the time of union, defined and extended; stations were arranged in districts for the first time in 1861. In 1863, too, a scheme was adopted for directing the studies of junior preachers, and arrangements were made for their 'examination by printed questions'. In 1867 a 'Chapel Loan Fund' was established to make interest-free loans to chapels, whereas the previous, very inadequate, Chapel Fund made small grants.

Ministerial training started off rather slowly; there were still for a long time the prejudices against it that had obtained in 1835.[13] The question was raised, however, in 1860, when a committee was appointed to prepare a

[13] Concern was felt by some lest the students should lose their piety and zeal, and become proud. That latter tendency—if it were there at all—would no doubt be dispelled in the case of one student who, failing to produce a sermon for the Friday criticism class, was instructed to provide one for the following Friday on the text: 'I do remember my faults this day.' (G. G. Hornby, *The Methodist College, Victoria Park, Manchester: A Souvenir* (n.d.), p. 6.)

scheme 'to assist the literary and theological training of the candidates';[14] but though the committee met and made recommendations to the next year's Assembly,[15] nothing happened for several years. In 1867 the matter was raised again, and in 1869 a report, in almost the same words as that of eight years before, was adopted. This provided for the setting apart of a minister in Manchester, who should take a number of students under his roof and train them, besides arranging for some of them to attend classes at Owen's College (now Manchester University). The students were to pay fees (which could if necessary be remitted), and the Tutor and students would be available for preaching-appointments, the fees from these to go to meet the Institute's expenses. An alternative suggestion was put forward, that accepted candidates should live by twos and threes in the homes of senior ministers; but the Assembly adopted the bold course. The Institute was opened with six students under Thomas Hacking as Principal, in a hired house in Stockport Road in September 1872, moving in 1877 to a building converted from three dwelling-houses in Victoria Park, which was enlarged in the last years of the century. This College continued to serve Methodism in the UMFC, the United Methodist Church, and finally the united Methodism, till 1934. It had been urged that the very man who was one of the keenest exponents of the scheme, Richard Chew, was himself the best argument against it, for *he* had had no formal training. Marmaduke Miller perhaps summed the matter up best when he wrote in a long letter to the *Magazine* in 1861: 'If God has no need of our learning, He has still less need of our ignorance.'[16] The same year that the Institute opened, the venerable James Everett died at the age of eighty-eight, and his library and museum were purchased for the Institute; these were more of antiquarian than practical value, but their preservation in that way was a worthy memorial to the man who, rebel though he was, loved Methodism passionately. It was a strange coincidence

[14] *Minutes* (1860), p. 50.   [15] ibid. (1861), p. 56.   [16] op. cit. p. 435.

that Everett, the expelled, and Thomas Jackson, the President who expelled him, should be the two men who, more than any other, invented the hobby of Wesleyana-collecting! Unhappily, the last eighty years, with all their changes, have seen the gradual disappearance of most of Everett's collections.

Closely allied, in purpose, to ministerial training, is a good education for the children of ministers and others; and the matter had been considered as early as 1844, a committee being appointed to go into the question. But the idea died out, and the subject was not reopened till 1875 when the Assembly decided to establish a school. Almost immediately an estate in Harrogate came into the market, and Ashville College, as it was, and still is called, was opened in 1877. Meanwhile, another step had been taken in 1876, when a London Home Mission Scheme was submitted and approved.

Two years later a number of memorials were sent to the Assembly in favour of a Connexional Temperance Organization, and in 1880 the 'Free Methodist Temperance League' was consequently founded. But temperance feeling had long been strong in the Connexion. The second Assembly of the Wesleyan Association in 1837 had passed a strong resolution urging all members to encourage the various temperance societies in the Kingdom; and this and similar resolutions figure frequently in the succeeding years. Indeed, the Free Methodists took a leading part in advocating total abstinence and restrictions on 'hours of opening'. In Cornwall and Yorkshire, amalgamations took place of independent societies and circuits which had teetotal principles; thus in 1842 various Methodist churches in Hayle who had been known as the 'Temperance Methodists', had amalgamated with the Association. About the same year, a group called the 'Teetotal Methodists' opened a chapel in Camborne, and later this little cause became part of the Association.[17] Similarly about 1849 or 1850 the Christian Temperance Brethren, worshipping in Bethel Chapel, Leeds, became merged

[17] *Magazine* (1864), p. 48.

into an early Wesleyan Reform society.[18] Temperance Street Chapel in Elland, Yorkshire, carries its history in its name; and Sowerby Providence Chapel, built in 1875, was a break-away from the Wesleyans on the same question of whether a Band of Hope was a desirable auxiliary to a Methodist society.[19] Furthermore, it was reported in 1859 that all the twelve candidates for ordination were teetotal, and by 1896 almost every one of the 370 ministers was an abstainer. It is not surprising then that two years after the formation of the Temperance League, in 1882, its secretary, John Thornley, was freed from circuit duties to give his entire time and energies to the prosecution of the work; and the Free Methodists could be proud of the fact that they were the first Christian communion to set a minister apart for the task.

Nor was temperance, narrowly understood, their sole interest. Indeed, most of the concerns of the Christian Citizenship Department of today were the concerns of our Free Methodist fathers. Already in 1840 the Assembly had resolved 'that this Meeting, believing that War is contrary to the spirit of the Gospel, and highly injurious both to the bodies and souls of men, cordially approves of the "Peace Society" and sincerely prays for its success'.[20] A generation later the Assembly rejoiced in the passing of Mr Henry Richard's resolution in the House of Commons in favour of a 'general and permanent system of international arbitration';[21] and resolutions on arbitration figure frequently in the *Minutes* in the 1890's onward. Nor did their opposition to slavery swerve when the cotton famine, resultant upon the Civil War, threw immense numbers in Lancashire into unemployment. And it was the lecturing campaign of a Free Methodist minister, the eloquent John Guttridge, in that period, which helped more than anything else to keep Lancashire patient and sympathetic toward freedom for the slaves, notwithstanding the famine.

[18] ibid. (1862), p. 719.
[19] E. V. Chapman, *John Wesley and Company (Halifax)* (Halifax 1952), p. 72.
[20] *Minutes* (1840), p. 20.   [21] *Magazine* (1873), pp. 502, 562.

One of the outstanding features of church life a century ago—no doubt it was common to many branches of Christ's Church—was the passion for tea-meetings, followed by a galaxy of speakers. The references in the 'circuit intelligence' to 'the cup that cheers but not inebriates' become positively tiresome! Everything was celebrated with a tea-meeting; the Amalgamation culminated in a gathering when nearly a thousand people took tea together, and the after-meeting was attended by some 1,500 persons. The capacity of our forefathers for listening appreciatively to many and long speeches shames us. 'There were giants in the earth in those days' —nor was their presence restricted to the platform! When the foundation stone of Orchard Chapel, Preston (recently closed), was laid in August 1861, there was a tea-meeting followed by six speakers, which lasted till eleven o'clock! When a chapel in Leeds was opened in 1863, there were ten speeches between the tea and a quarter past ten. At the opening meeting of Kehelland Chapel, Redruth, in 1862, there were many speakers, one of whom, Joseph Colman, spoke for two hours. Chapel stone-layings, openings, Sunday-school Anniversaries, missionary anniversaries—all were celebrated with tea and an evening of speeches. Nor were the speakers all of their own denomination. Indeed, the catholicity—or should one in these days say, rather, ecumenicity?—of the Free Methodists of last century is amazing. We do our fathers a grave injustice when we suggest, as we so often do, that they were a prejudiced, intolerant crowd. The Free Methodists were certainly not noted for flabbiness of opinion; they were among the keenest supporters of the Liberation Society for the separation of Church and State, and for a long while they remembered Buntingism and regretted that some traces of it were still left among the Conference Methodists; but all this makes the catholicity of their platforms the more notable. At Red Lion Street, Clerkenwell, Sunday-school Anniversary in 1859, it was the Curate of neighbouring St James's who moved the adoption of the report in a speech valuable 'for Christian catholicity and appropriateness to education of a Scriptural character'.[22] When John Guttridge left Preston in 1859, there were nine speeches from 'men of nearly every denomination',[23] in addition to Guttridge's own reply. When Trinity Road Chapel, Bristol, was reopened, the chair at the meeting was taken by a neighbouring rector;[24] at the 1854 Assembly at Rochdale, other evangelical ministers shared the luncheon table, including the Wesleyan minister, who spoke—and this was only five years after 1849! When Preston Orchard Chapel was opened in 1862, the Wesleyan Superintendent of the Preston Circuit preached one of the sermons on the first Sunday;[25] at the May Missionary Meeting in 1873 in Exeter Hall, Luke Wiseman, then President of the Wesleyan Conference, was a speaker, and 'was received with loud and continued cheering';[26] and it was a Baptist minister who laid the stone of a chapel at Hathern in the Loughborough Circuit.[27] Examples of this brotherly feeling are legion, and are sufficient to demolish for good our mistaken ideas of the 'bitterness' of last century. But the crowning example was related in the 1862 *Magazine* by a correspondent from Wisbech, who wrote: 'At Thorney Toll, the chapel was filled to overflowing [for the Missionary Meeting], the vicar of Thorney having consented to preside at our meeting ... the vicar, in compliance with my request about six months ago, very kindly consented to have his name put on our Circuit Plan, where it now stands, and to take four Sabbath appointments in each quarter, besides an appointment on weekdays every fortnight.'[28] Could that happen even in *these* enlightened days? A writer in the 1860 *Magazine* truly says: 'We do not think the existence of different sections [of Christ's Church] is an evil, or that their being merged in one would infallibly secure a great revival. It is not the existence of sects that hinders a revival, but the existence of sectarianism.'[29]

[22] *Magazine* (1859), p. 392.   [23] ibid. p. 561.   [24] ibid. (1860), p. 703.
[25] ibid. (1862), p. 537.   [26] ibid. (1873), p. 359.   [27] ibid. (1863), p. 463.
[28] op. cit. p. 265.   [29] op cit. p. 532.

As Methodists, the Free Churches were committed to evangelism; and it is a slur on their reputation to suggest that they only grew by accessions of dissidents. While their early magazines deal trenchantly with matters of Church government, they did not forget their main purpose—'to save souls'. Was not the magazine which Samuel Dunn refused to suspend called the *Wesley Banner and Revival Record*? And when Matthew Baxter spoke at the meeting in Nottingham to celebrate the amalgamation there in 1859 between Reformers and Associationists, he said: 'They must stand firmly by those principles which were the sheet-anchor of their freedom; but they must ever give the greatest prominence to evangelical objects. Their great mission was to *save souls*, and to diffuse evangelical truth. Objects like these transcended in their importance all merely organic and ecclesiastical objects.'[30] And when one reads the magazines of the period when their championship of principles was most intransigent, one is struck by the real passion for evangelism that filled our forefathers. Nor was it a question of special missioners, though they were certainly made use of, and James Caughey, the American revivalist, found no warmer supporters in England than among the Free Methodists;[31] the question was even raised of placing his name somewhere on the 'stations', so that it might be evident that he had the approval of the Assembly,[32] which he was invited to address in 1857.[33] 'Protracted meetings' were a favourite means of evangelism. At Bacup such meetings continued for nine weeks after the chapel reopening,[34] and resulted in 300 conversions. New Mills employed a local preacher for four weeks, which led to the circuit being independent of connexional funds for the first time.[35] But often the agencies were the local workers. The Sheffield Mount Tabor Circuit arranged a week's revival services in most places in the circuit, conducted by the ministers

---

[30] *Magazine* (1859), p. 165.
[31] Townsend, Workman, and Eayrs, *New History of Methodism*, I.545.
[32] *Minutes* (1861), p. 60.   [33] *Minutes* (1857), p. 54.
[34] *Magazine* (1862), pp. 51-2.   [35] ibid. (1861), pp. 460-1.

and local preachers.[36] Kingswood reported a revival in the same year, resulting in 'several hundreds' being converted, without any special agency; in Newcastle-under-Lyme and Longton, an extensive revival took place through the preaching of a converted navvy;[37] Scarborough reported great prosperity and increase without any of the 'excitement of novelty';[38] Barnsley told of a Sunday-school trip at which the company were singing 'My God is reconciled, His pardoning voice I hear', when a woman in the carriage was convicted through the singing, and the Methodists present got down on their knees and held a prayer-meeting in the railway carriage till the woman obtained pardon and peace;[39] and Penzance told in 1862 how William Booth (who had left the New Connexion the previous year) had spent some time in the circuit, resulting in 150 conversions and others who claimed the blessing of entire sanctification.[40] Often many other churches shared in the increase in members. Such stories as these are constantly being told, resulting in the glad announcement of deserted public houses and chapels uncomfortably full.

Later in the century, the Free Methodists joined in the Central Mission movement, and from 1889 Lady Lane Chapel, Leeds, became a Central Mission, rather than an ordinary circuit chapel.

No Methodists could exist long without having to deal with Trust problems! And the problems were naturally particularly acute in a community which had a passion for local independence and which at the same time was trying to live as a connexion. Model deeds were a case in point. In the earliest days, many chapels were on private deeds, but it was soon found necessary to draw up a connexional deed, so as to secure the property to the Connexion. In consequence, a 'Model Deed' was drafted by the Association in 1842. There were constant complaints that many trusts were fighting shy of it, and after the Union of 1857 another deed was drafted, in 1865, known as the 'Reference Deed'; the purpose of this was to make the

---

[36] ibid. (1862), p. 62.   [37] ibid. p. 329.   [38] ibid. p. 330.
[39] ibid. (1860), p. 62.   [40] ibid. (1862), p. 725.

deed as acceptable as possible to local sentiment. The principles and arrangements of both are almost identical,[41] the main difference being that under the latter Deed any person, though not a Church member, might be appointed as a trustee, if approved by the Quarterly Meeting; whereas under the Model Deed, no one was eligible who was not a member of the UMFC. The Reference Deed thus gave local Free Methodists the maximum freedom of choice. But in either case, the Deeds ensured that the chapels were to be used for public worship according to the doctrines and usages of the UMFC, and gave the Assembly the right to the first offer for the property if it became necessary to sell it. They ensured that the property was not diverted from its proper use, while allowing trustees an 'uncontrolled discretion in the conduct of the Trust';[42] the income too had to be devoted to Free Methodist purposes, and individual trustees were covered if they had lent money to the trust. Even so, by 1898 only 757 out of a total of 1,249 chapels were connexionally settled.[43]

This extreme independence led to very poor support for the Connexional Chapel Fund; in 1860 the total income was only £145.[44] But no church was likely to support that fund if it could never benefit from it, and no church could benefit from it if it were not settled connexionally. John Cuthbertson, a leading London layman, suggested that help might be given provided chapels were settled on trusts and not privately owned.[45] But the upshot was the formation of a new fund, a 'Chapel Loan Fund', that could lend money free of interest, provided it were repaid over a period of years and that an annual grant to the Fund were made. This fund did yeoman service for many years in reducing chapel debts.

One other feature is interesting. Frequently in the

---

[41] An interesting tabular comparison of the provisions of various Model Deeds is found in E. Benson Perkins, *Methodist Preaching Houses and the Law* (WHS Lecture, 1952), pp. 88ff. The similarity is remarkable.

[42] E. Askew, *Free Methodist Manual* (London 1899), p. 239.

[43] ibid. p. 262.

[44] *Magazine* (1861), p. 95.   [45] ibid. p. 165.

early days chapels were built on the shareholding principle. This was true of a place like Baillie Street, Rochdale; the chapel and school were financed by means of an issue of shares and a prospectus was issued. At the first annual meeting of shareholders in July 1837 it was resolved that a dividend of £5 per cent per annum be paid, and a further £2½ per cent was paid in 1840. Baillie Street must be one of the few chapels that have paid a cash dividend! The experiment ended in 1841, as most such experiments ended, by the settling of the chapel on the Connexion, the shareholders relinquishing their shares, and subscriptions being solicited to repay those shareholders who were not in a financial position to do so.[46]

Finally, the Free Methodists also engaged in deaconess activities. Following, presumably, the lead of the Wesleyans, who had established a Deaconess Order in 1890, Messrs J. A. and S. Bowron gave furniture, costumes and money to start a Free Methodist Deaconess Institute in memory of their father William Bowron, of London. A house was taken in Lupus Street, Pimlico, and opened in April 1891 with Thomas B. Saul as tutor and Thomas J. Cope as secretary—both in addition to their circuit duties! The Institute was more familiarly known as 'Bowron House' and the deaconesses as 'Bowron House Sisters'. It continued into the United Methodist Church after 1907, and was finally closed in 1935 when all deaconess work was centred at the ex-Wesleyan Deaconess College at Ilkley.[47]

---

[46] E. C. Cryer, *A Centenary History of the Methodist Church, Baillie Street, Rochdale* (Rochdale 1937), pp. 22ff.
[47] cf. Askew, op. cit., pp. 384ff.; and the *Methodist Recorder* for 16th October 1952, p. 3.

IV

FREE

THE SCENE is Bristol in 1859. The stone is being laid of a new United Methodist Free Church in Portwall Lane; William Reed, one of the circuit ministers, who was destined to become President three years later, has laid the stone and is now speaking. ' "One is your master, even Christ",' he quotes, ' "and all ye are brethren." It is the privilege [of the United Churches] to rejoice in a constitution which, without degrading the ministry, secures the freedom of the people. The two great features by which the ecclesiastical system of the United Churches is distinguished, we take to be unfettered representation in the annual assembly, or conference of the body, and circuit independence in relation to all local matters. Except in reference to the itinerancy, to which many of the circuits are warmly attached, the Annual Assembly possesses no legislative power, and we think that, without disparaging other systems, it may be truthfully affirmed that the members of the Methodist Free Churches enjoy, in its most comprehensive sense, that liberty with which Christ makes His people free.'[1]

That scene was repeated a multitude of times. Whenever a chapel was being opened or its foundation stone laid, whenever after 1857 a Reform circuit was contemplating amalgamation, that was the theme *par excellence*. The speaker might speak of many things—he generally did, in fact, speak of the doctrines to be preached in the chapel—but that subject was sure to come in. And it is worth noting that these very lay opinions were being uttered enthusiastically by ministers. 'Free Representation and Local Independence'—these were the watchwords that rang out time and time again in the speeches,

[1] *Magazine* (1859), p. 221.

sermons, articles, reports, of the Free Methodists; they were the twin foundation stones of their ecclesiastical edifice.

The gibe has sometimes been cast that they were more Free than Methodist; and no doubt they sometimes were. It would be a miracle if in no place and on no occasion did liberty run to licence. It would be a miracle if the other watchword, the watchword of the Reformation, that appeared on the title-page of their magazine from 1838 onwards: 'The right of private judgement in the reading of the Sacred Volume', did not lead to a wrong judgement on occasion. But the last chapter has perhaps served to show how truly Methodist they were, in spite of their freedom.

'Free Representation'—that was the first watchword. They had suffered at the hands of a Conference that was entirely ministerial and that sat behind closed doors, a conference which was composed, legally, of the senior ministers of the body together with those whom those ministers themselves might elect. 'A Conference of the *People called Methodists?*' said they. 'Not at all.' Consequently their Assembly had only four *ex officio* members: the President, Connexional Secretary, Corresponding Secretary, and Connexional Treasurer of the previous year. All the other members were elected by the circuits, the number to be elected varying according to the size of the circuit. The circuits were entitled to elect whom they would; it might be a minister, it might not. There was no compulsion to elect their superintendent, not even if he were Chairman of the District (and the Chairman was not necessarily a minister, in any case); and there were occasions when the Chairman was *not* elected. In point of fact, after the first few years of the amalgamation, when laymen were in a slight majority simply because the bulk of Reform circuits had no minister, the ministers were usually in a majority; the lack of guaranteed places did not react unfairly on them; they were elected, not of right, but because they were esteemed 'very highly in love for their work's sake'. It was the circuits, not the districts,

E

that elected representatives; and in practice what normally happened was that in a one-man circuit the minister went in alternate years, in a two-man circuit, one minister and one layman were the representatives. But that was simply how things generally worked out. Difficulties arose when men began to be set apart from circuit duties for specialized work. The General Missionary Secretary was released from circuit work in 1864, the Editor and Book Steward (a combined office) in 1869, the Principal of the Theological Institute in 1872, the Secretary of the Chapel Fund (and certain other funds) in 1873, and the Temperance Secretary in 1882. None of these was *ex officio* a member of the Assembly; in all the fifty years of its existence as a denomination, the total number of *ex officio* members was never increased. The result was that these additional departmental officials had to take their chance. They often got round the difficulty in a novel way. When the Assembly met, the first thing done, after opening devotions, was the examination of the certificates accrediting the various representatives. On two or three occasions a man was appointed by a circuit in which he was not resident; James Everett, resident in Newcastle, was once appointed by the Diss Circuit; Matthew Baxter of Heywood claimed in 1864 to represent Scarborough; and Thomas Hacking, the Theological Tutor of Manchester, claimed in 1873 to represent Truro. The question arose as to whether these were valid appointments. Technically 'membership in the body' alone constituted the legal qualification; on the other hand, it was urged that the way the rule had been interpreted by those who framed it was the real guide; and in the first twenty years after the Foundation Deed had been drawn up, no man had ever represented a circuit other than that where he lived. It was ultimately decided that that should be the normal interpretation; but that those officers who had not a circuit to appoint them should be eligible for appointment by any circuit.[2] Thus in 1907 Henry T. Chapman, the Foreign Missionary Secretary, represented Wenchow.

[2] cf. for instance *Minutes* (1861), p. 3; *Magazine* (1873), p. 526.

Until that was decided the normal procedure was to allow department officials to sit in the Assembly, and to speak if necessary, but not to vote.[3]

'Local Independence'—that was the other foundation stone which could not be moved. The great matter at issue in 1827 and later was how far the Conference could move without local concurrence, and especially how far it could legislate for local affairs. Hence great care was taken, in drawing up the Foundation Deed in 1840, which became after 1857 the Foundation Deed of the United Churches, to state the precise functions and limitations of the Annual Assembly. These are summed up in an article in the 1853 *Magazine*[4] by Joah Mallinson, a leading Leeds Associationist. Some had misunderstood the Foundation Deed, so he sought to answer the questions: What is the extent of the authority of the Assembly? and What are the inalienable rights of the circuits? The Assembly, he summed up, had rights; rights over the minister and rights to withhold permission to divide circuits, to apply connexional funds and manage the Book Room, to appoint connexional officers, to arrange terms of union with other circuits and churches, to fix the date of the next Assembly and determine who is eligible to be present, to appoint rules for the government of its own proceedings, to withdraw itself from any circuit which is corrupt in doctrine, and so on.[5] Thus while no circuit had absolute independence, neither had the Assembly. On the other hand, every circuit had the right to admit and expel members and administer its internal affairs, to elect and send members to the Assembly, to reject modifications in the Foundation Deed,[6] to recommend preachers for the itinerancy (no preachers being admitted

---

[3] cf. for instance *Minutes* (1866), p. 8.   [4] pp. 471ff.

[5] This is amplified in a regulation of 1894 (*Minutes*, p. 213), where it is pointed out that if the Connexion has the right to withdraw itself from any church or circuit, that right necessarily carried with it the right of investigation and inquiry. So that when there is a *prima facie* case, the circuit is constitutionally bound to permit the investigation.

[6] This of course is similar to our present-day regulation for 'Provisional Leglislation'.

other than by the recommendation of the circuit, society, or church meeting), and to invite ministers, subject to the approval of the Assembly. The Foundation Deed made it all plain in the addendum to that paragraph which provided for the terms of the Deed to be altered every tenth year if necessary—a wise precaution that prevented the constant adjusting of the constitution that leaves a church uncertain of what the law is. As Robert Eckett remarked in the 1858 Assembly: 'Once in ten years is quite often enough to make a new Constitution.' 'Or to repair an old one', interjected Matthew Baxter. The addendum is worth quoting in full:

Provided always that nothing herein contained shall authorize, or be construed to authorize, the said Annual Assembly, or the Itinerant preachers to suspend or expel any non-Itinerant, usually called Local preachers, Steward, Leader or other member of the said Association; the Circuit, Society, or Church meetings, and authorities, constituted according to the custom or rule of each such Circuit possessing the exclusive power of suspending and expelling all such persons; or whereby the doctrines of the said Association hereinbefore stated or referred to, shall or may be altered or controverted by the said Annual Assembly; or whereby the said Assembly shall, or may become a non-elective or self-elective body; or whereby the right of freely electing and sending representatives annually as aforesaid, may be destroyed or impeded; or whereby Itinerant, non-Itinerant usually called Local preachers, or other official or private members of the said Association may be precluded from being elected and sent as representatives. And it is hereby declared that all minutes or resolutions, acts or proceedings, for effecting all or any of such prohibited purposes, shall be absolutely void and inoperative.[7]

Mallinson went on to urge that these terms could satisfy even the most rabid Reformers, 'some of whom boast of being greatly ahead of the Association, in having a "cheap gospel" and more of their Scriptural rights'; though some were more far-seeing, one of their 'chief men' having remarked: 'The fact is, that it is so difficult to have a

[7] *Minutes* (1840), p. 45.

connexion at all, and yet to preserve an absolute independence in each circuit, and in every church, that it will be
with us some day a question that will involve serious
discussion and, I should be afraid, serious embarrassments
also.'[8] In the same magazine, Robert Eckett deals with
a suggestion made in the *Wesleyan Times*, that the Association, the Reformers, and the New Connexion should
amalgamate; he points out that the Reformers repudiate
the authority of any conference, and the New Connexion
'repudiates circuit independence'. 'In the Connexion to
which I belong, we think we have solved the problem of
combining proper circuit independency with the advan-
tages of Connexionalism.'[9] Eckett was of course the chief
architect of the Foundation Deed.

How did this work out? It may be worth while quoting
one or two incidents. In 1873, two chapels withdrew
from Sheffield Mount Tabor Circuit, and the Connexional
Committee recommended compliance with their request
to be constituted a separate circuit. Some argued that
this was a secession and not a division of circuit in the
sense contemplated by the regulation; the Assembly had
previously reserved the right to be consulted before local
action was taken, and therefore the Assembly should not
give its sanction. But the Assembly voted 'by a large
majority' for the right of the circuit to divide itself.[10]

A different sort of case arose in 1864. Captain King, a
leading London layman, brought a complaint that the
Assembly had placed a young brother as superintendent
of the London Third Circuit over one who was his senior
in age. The circuit had taken no action because they
loyally regarded the Assembly as the highest authority,
and did not feel free to alter what it had done. William
Reed, an ex-President, and then Editor and Book Steward,
pointed out in reply that all that the Assembly had done
was to make the man responsible for passing on to his
circuit communications on connexional affairs—'Every
circuit could elect its own chairman'.[11]

[8] *Magazine* (1853), pp. 471ff.   [9] ibid. p. 413.
[10] ibid. (1873), p. 512.   [11] ibid. (1864), p. 551.

As early as 1837 the Assembly of the Association resolved 'that as we believe that those who are called by Christ to preach the Gospel, and who render their services gratuitously, are not thereby less qualified to exercise any of the offices of the Christian Ministry than those who are maintained by the contributions of the Church; they, therefore, are eligible to be appointed by the Quarterly Meeting of the Societies, to discharge any of the offices of the Christian Ministry';[12] it is worthy of note that the resolution couples the priesthood of all believers with the freedom of quarterly meetings to make their own regulations. This meant of course that local preachers—or indeed any approved layman—were qualified to conduct both the Sacramental services. It is difficult to imagine a layman ever doing so when a minister was present; but the rule did mean that village chapels could enjoy the privilege more frequently than would otherwise have been the case. They held that if a person were acceptable to the local flock of Christ, his administering of the Sacraments was no concern of any who were not being called on to accept them at his hands.

Furthermore, a 'free' (i.e. non-liturgical) mode of Sacramental Service was characteristic of the Free Methodists; the preacher conducted the service extempore, normally including in it a brief address and often giving opportunity to others to lead in prayer, as in a prayer meeting. Stewards normally distributed the elements, having received them from the preacher.[13] (This form of worship was no doubt one of the many things that Free Methodism owed to the Congregationalists, who beamed upon the UMFC with especial benediction.) In many places, too, members were issued with booklets of twelve Sacramental tickets yearly; and the surrender of a ticket at the service showed who had been present. All this of course indicates that a keen appreciation of the Sacrament is

[12] *Minutes* (1837), p. 24. cf. also Wm. Boyden and Edwin Askew: *Handbook of the UMFC* (2nd ed. London 1887, p. 3): 'Baptism and the Lord's Supper . . . are administered by preachers, itinerant or local.'
[13] cf. Leeds Lady Lane Circuit Rules (p. 6): 'The [Leaders'] meeting shall likewise appoint suitable persons to assist in the distribution of the elements of bread and wine at the ordinance of the Lord's Supper.'

not restricted to High Churchmen and liturgiologists!
In 1861 the Bridgwater Circuit appointed as its pastor
a man who was not a UMFC minister. There was some
strong feeling in the Assembly, one member even proposing that Bridgwater be no longer recognized. But it was
pointed out that 'any circuit not having one of our
ministers, but contributing to our funds', was in fellowship with the Free Churches.[14]

In 1859 the important Louth Circuit, with some 1600
members, amalgamated with the UMFC. They were so
independent that they had held aloof from the Wesleyan
Reformers, and only joined the Free Churches because they
were at last convinced of the value of amalgamation—it
would, for instance, enable them to take part in Overseas
and Home Missions enterprises, and it would give them
a wider freedom in their choice of ministers. At the circuit
meeting called to discuss the matter (preceded as a matter
of course by a tea at which 700 sat down), they invited
Robert Eckett, then President, to address them on the
constitution of the UMFC, and then questioned him; and
the report of that meeting is one of the most interesting
summaries of the Free Methodists' polity.[15] What is
significant is that local independence was such that
even as late as 1871 they continued to issue their own
class-tickets, headed: 'Free Methodist Church. Louth
Circuit.'

We have already noted that District Meetings were
established in 1857. They had at first a very restricted
function. Free representation was again the order of the
day; but in course of time some *ex officio* members were
added, such as the various District officials, Connexional
officials, members of Connexional Committees, and supernumerary ministers. But it was expressly stated that 'only
such circuits as approve of District Meetings will be
expected to appoint a representative or representatives to
attend them; and no District Meeting shall have authority
to interfere in the affairs of a circuit, unless advice, or other
interference has been requested by the Circuit Quarterly

14 *Magazine* (1861), p. 543.   15 ibid. (1859), pp. 507ff.

Meeting'.[16] Although the Convener was appointed by the Assembly, the May meeting elected its own chairman and other officials, and those appointments were final. The functions of District Meetings were at first restricted to carrying out the resolutions of the Assembly, promoting the prosperity of the Work of God in the district, and rendering assistance to such circuits as requested it;[17] but they gradually increased, till at the close of the denomination's history, they served as a sort of clearing-house, so that reports and schedules went first to the meeting for classification before being sent to the connexional officers.

Local independence of another sort is seen in the fact that from an early date groups of churches outside England, forming part of the UMFC, had their own assemblies. We have seen references to the 'Scottish United Methodist Churches' in the first *Minutes* of the Association from 1836 onward. Though their Stations were listed in the *Minutes*, and their ministers regarded as belonging to the body, these Scottish Churches had their own Assembly to which the Association sent representatives,[18] and for some years Annual Addresses were passed between the two bodies. In the same way the Jamaica Association had its own Assembly and received and sent Addresses to Britain. By 1861 the United Welsh Societies had a Moderator, and indeed a layman held the office for several years;[19] and when the Australian work had developed, the appointments there were made by the local Annual Assemblies.

Was there a weakness in all this liberty? On the whole, no. The Connexion continued to grow, both by amalgamations and by normal processes. Secessions did occasionally occur, but very rarely; and the possibility had been envisaged.[20] The membership which in 1857 had been 39,986, had risen to 81,444 forty years later, and to 90,870 by 1907, with 12,333 on trial. That does not spell weakness or defeat. But there were clearly weaknesses—the weaknesses always inherent in liberty. There was only one compulsory connexional collection, that for

---

[16] *Minutes* (1857), p. 19.   [17] ibid. p. 21.   [18] ibid. (1836), pp. 19, 24.
[19] *Magazine* (1861), p. 454.   [20] cf. for example, *Magazine* (1859), p. 511.

the Home and Foreign Missionary Fund. Hence there were frequent complaints that the other funds were not adequately supported. Joseph Kirsop noted that, for instance, the Theological Institute was inadequately supported from the first.[21] He proposed therefore a constitutional amendment whereby a second compulsory Sunday's collection should be levied, to be allocated by the Assembly to the different funds.[22]

Another effect of circuit independence—or rather the spirit of independence—was the tendency for some circuits to split up into smaller circuits with only one or two churches each. They became for all intents and purposes Congregational churches. This was a real weakness as they had not then the measure of connexional sense that comes from being attached to several other societies in a normal circuit. Concentration of ministerial labour led to a weakening of strength—a moral we might well take to heart today, when so many think 'concentration' is the panacea. It is of course the very denial of that essential principle of a Connexion, that the strong help the weak. And in 1898, out of a total of 234 circuits, forty-two were one-church, and twenty-eight two-church circuits. The result of this tendency was a regulation passed in 1891, expressing concern that so many small places had been given up, and reminding ministers that they were appointed to a *circuit*, and should not, therefore, neglect the smaller places. The reminder is still timely.

No, the liberty was not on the whole abused. Liberty to elect a lay President led to only two such in the fifty years from 1857 to 1907, viz. Sir James Duckworth and Mr H. T. Mawson; and liberty to elect laymen or ministers to the Assembly resulted in a slight majority of ministers in most years, in spite of William Reed's remark in 1864, that he had 'yet to learn, that it was right or expedient, that two hundred ministers should be as strongly represented in the Annual Assembly as 63,000 members and local preachers'.[23]

[21] Kirsop, *Historic Sketches of Free Methodism*, p. 67.
[22] ibid.   [23] *Magazine* (1864), p. 555.

V

THEIR WORLD PARISH

I. IRELAND, WALES AND SCOTLAND

IT IS NOT so long since a distinguished Methodist historian confessed to the present writer that he had had no idea that the United Methodist Free Churches ever had work in Scotland; and no doubt he is not alone. But they had work in Ireland and Wales too.

The first two Assemblies of the Wesleyan Association saw the presence of a representative from Carrickfergus. That place (with thirteen members in 1837) early received help in the shape of collections taken throughout the Connexion for its chapel, Rochdale responding magnificently with nearly £70. Its numbers, never large, fluctuated seriously—for instance, the sixty-two reported in 1851 were reduced to twenty-seven the following year. More than once the mission was referred to the 'serious consideration' of the Connexional Committee, which was empowered to take whatever action it deemed expedient.[1] In 1864 it was proposed, unsuccessfully, by that Committee to discontinue the mission,[2] and the following year an attempt was made to strengthen the work by opening up Belfast, the joint membership thus soaring to ninety. Belfast apparently flourished for a time and in 1866 the ninety had increased to 151. But next year it dropped to eighty-four, in spite of a small church at Ligoniel amalgamating with the other two. In 1868 the experiment was tried of joining Belfast to Carrickfergus, and appointing a second man to Ligoniel, but in the following year an appointment was made to Belfast only, the other places being discontinued. Finally, in 1872, the Belfast

---

[1] e.g. in *Minutes* (1862), p. 56.

[2] ibid. (1864), p. 62; *Magazine* (1864), pp. 559-60.

Society with sixty-eight members withdrew from the Connexion.[3] So came to an end the story of a struggling mission.

Wales too had a share in the attentions of the Free Methodists. By the second Association Assembly, there was a representative from Ruabon (later for years known as Overton, near Wrexham), which reported 301 members. In 1841 a group of Churches known as the 'Welsh Independent Methodists' amalgamated, with thirteen chapels and five other preaching-places. Altogether, at various times before 1857, the following places appear in the *Minutes*: Liverpool, Wrexham, Holywell, Tryddyn (Flints), Harwood, Rhos, Llanarchragag, Bodedryn, Glasenfryn, Tryddyn (Anglesey), Lleyn (including Rhun, Llanjian, and Llanbedrof), Aberystwyth, Bangor, Denbigh, Towyn, and Dolgelly, in addition to Overton, and a place spelt 'Eisingwge' (attached to Bodedryn)—but it is difficult to know from the spelling which places are intended in some cases!

They were recognized as a group on their own, had an Annual Assembly of their own, with a 'Moderator',[4] and often sent an Address to the Assembly, to which one of their ministers (never more than five in all) went as a representative. Perhaps because of the need of one who could speak English fluently, that man was often Griffith Griffiths. His Addresses, delivered with typical Welsh fervour—he would burst into Welsh in the middle!—were something of an event in the Assembly, were normally printed in the *Magazine* in full, and were sometimes ordered to be printed and circulated throughout the Connexion. The following is a fair specimen of his style:

Alas! Some of our brethren are dead, and have been lost to our Churches at home and abroad. I am on the wing;[5] but no blasts in my face shall hinder my flight to the mount of God. While the tear starts from my eyes from affection to my departed friends, triumph rises from my heart from a belief in their felicity. One said to an aged friend: 'I have had a letter

[3] *Minutes* (1872), p. 104.   [4] See p. 72, *supra.*
[5] Is he referring to the Welsh 'hwyl'?

from a distant correspondent, who inquired whether you are in the land of the living.' 'No,' replied the venerable man; 'but I am going there.' This world is shadow; that which is to come is one living reality. Our days of mourning are well nigh at an end; but our happiness will be eternal. As for me, I shall come up through the wilderness leaning on my Beloved; He doeth all things according to the grandeur of a God.[6]

They were, however, generally in pecuniary difficulties, and regularly received a Home Mission grant in the neighbourhood of £100 per annum at first, but rising to £220 in 1872.

The year 1857 brought a new circuit of Wesleyan Reformers into the Connexion, at Merthyr Tydfil; but that place disappeared two years later. Similarly, Llangybi features for a few years from 1861; and the 'Tabular View' of 1866 attributes the serious drop in that year to the secession of one society and to the fact that what we should now call 'junior members' had previously been included in the total. For the rest of their history, the same places figure in the stations, though sometimes re-grouped in new circuit alignments. New places are Broughton, Oswestry, and Pentre, and from time to time places dropped out. Later on, the status of these causes as the 'Welsh Mission' gave way to their inclusion in the normal way among the circuits of the Liverpool and Northwich District. By the early 1890's, the erstwhile mission had only one minister in charge of all its circuits; Poolmouth (the new name for the Wrexham area churches) was under the care of the Liverpool Central minister, and only Overton stood thoroughly on its own feet. The General Missionary Secretary had nominal oversight of some of the churches ten years later; but the little cause at Bodedryn with twenty-seven members withdrew in 1904; and at Union, in 1907, the Tryddyn Circuit, with three chapels and 123 members, was transferred to the Welsh Calvinistic Methodists. So the circuits entering that union were cut down to Overton, Poolmouth, and Aberystwyth.

[6] *Magazine* (1863), p. 581.

Scotland's story is much the same. There is no echo now of their existence there, for it is a lifetime since the last circuit closed down. Indeed, Scotland today has not so much as heard whether there be any United Methodism! But then the general ignorance that prevails in Scotland about Methodism is almost proverbial.[7] When the first Association Assembly met in 1836 there were three representatives from Scotland: Robert Anderson represented Edinburgh, and the 'Scottish United Methodist Churches' were represented by J. C. (sometimes printed C. J.) Kennedy and D. K. Shoebotham. These churches were clearly the results of earlier secessions, which had banded together and now allied themselves with the newly formed Association, though not completely merging for some years. From later Stations it seems that the 'Scottish UMC' stand for Paisley and Dundee, so that these two places and Edinburgh probably represented Free Methodism in the beginning. In the later years of the Association, Glasgow, Johnstone (near Paisley), Dumfries, Aberdeen, Kilmarnock were added to the original three, though there were never more than six towns represented at any one time.

In 1857 there was, as we should expect, an accession of strength, two Reform societies at Edinburgh and Glasgow joining the two remaining Association churches; but within two years Edinburgh alone remained, with a branch at Greenock which was given up in 1871; it had sixteen members. Reinforcements again arrived, in the shape of a society at Aberdeen with sixty-one members, which amalgamated with the UMFC in 1869, and a new Glasgow society in 1875 with 160 members, which increased to 210 two years later. The Aberdeen Church bought a fine, almost new, church in Dee Street in 1872 or early 1873 and requested help in the purchase of it.[8] But the old story repeated itself. Edinburgh disappeared

---

[7] This ignorance is illustrated in the question of the Brechin librarian when the present writer was seeking to track down the old Methodist Chapel there—'It would'na be the Cathedral ye're wanting? That's a fairly old building'!

[8] *Magazine* (1873), p. 49.

in 1880, Aberdeen in 1882, and the last, Glasgow, in 1884. Always in the Newcastle District, they had no doubt been too far removed from any others of like mind to be able to enjoy the sense of oneness that is Methodism's glory. There was never again any work north of the Wall. Every consideration appears to have been given by connexional authorities to Scotland's preference for a settled Ministry, for several men stationed there had tolerable tenures of office—Kennedy, for example, was minister in Paisley for twenty years. Although, then as now, far too many probationers were sent to that difficult field, they had the pick, so to speak; and many who worked there, such as T. A. Bayley, S. S. Barton, Thomas Newton, Robert Brewin, William Redfern, and John Peters, later became well-known names. The societies died out probably because of their smallness and remoteness; though Dundee seceded because of its independence, not wanting in anything to be subject to the Assembly. The societies were not burdened with capital debts, unlike many of Valentine Ward's societies,[9] because they often had preaching places only. (When 'chapels' are reported in the schedules, the reference is sometimes only to 'preaching-places', or even private houses. How else could Kilmarnock, with forty-eight members, report five preaching-places in 1842? No doubt the schedules were sometimes filled in wrongly!)[10]

Ireland, Wales, Scotland—all had Free Methodist societies and circuits, all of which died out apart from the three Welsh ones existing in 1907. The causes are only too easy to assess. In the first place, they suffered from isolation, and were cut off from the main stream of their Church's life. They could take little part in affairs outside their own circuits, and distance often meant that they were not represented at the Assembly. In the second place, they were very often left without ministerial oversight, to manage as best they could. In some cases their numbers,

[9] cf. Wesley Swift, *Methodism in Scotland, the First Hundred Years*, p. 85.
[10] cf. the writer's 'United Methodism in Scotland', in *WHS Proc.*, XXVIII.96ff.

from our point of view, did not justify a minister's being stationed. But it was the places where there was least strength whose need of help was greatest; the numbers never could improve until a man was stationed there. And in the third place, too often they were one-church circuits; they were in consequence drawn in upon themselves, and saw only their own difficulties and weakness; they would have been strengthened by a missionary outlook that was concerned to build up societies in the towns and villages of the neighbourhood. Self-centredness is fatal in church life as in private life. The result normally was death. Even now in 1957 we have not yet learnt these lessons.

II. OVERSEAS

As befits any Methodist community, from their earliest days the Free Methodists were engaged in overseas missionary enterprises. Not unnaturally, their first missionary fields were by the accession of fellow-dissidents. Mention has already been made of the Jamaican accessions,[11] but that field had an unhappy early history. Three men who were appointed to assist Thomas Pennock were lost to the work there—Kelsham Fullager, himself a Jamaican, died before the 1842 Assembly, and John Parkyn and Joseph Blythman, after being present at the emancipation of slaves in Jamaica, returned to England less than two years after their landing. A number of preachers in local connexion were added to the Stations, and in 1842 Matthew Baxter went out, remaining there nine years. There were disputes in the island, as a result of which, in spite of the Assembly's repeated attempts at reconciliation between Pennock and Baxter,[12] Pennock with the bulk of his members seceded in 1843, so that in 1845, 1,237 members only were reported. Preachers also seceded, and at one time Baxter was the only preacher on the island. Other men went out, notably William Griffith, who was

11 See p. 28 *supra*.
12 The Assembly was trying to reconcile them as late as 1848; see *Minutes* (1848), p. 34.

appointed in 1859 and stayed there for half a century; James Roberts, Elisha Penrose, and George Sanguinetti, too, remained there for a considerable period; and though after some years of decrease (in 1853 the membership was as low as 565), the membership gradually recovered, it never reached the figures it attained before the troubles of 1843; in 1907 the total was 3,890.

Progress was slow at all times. As always with new converts, and especially among emancipated slaves, morality was difficult to teach, necessitating frequent disciplinary measures.[13] Disaster, too, was not unknown. In 1880, for instance, a dreadful hurricane visited the island; James Roberts narrowly escaped death, and seventeen chapels were blown down. An appeal was made to the Connexion, resulting in almost £1,500 being specially raised for rehabilitation and relief.[14]

An offshoot of the Jamaica Mission was in Central America, where for many years there was a station at Bocas del Toro (an island off Panama), founded as a result of emigrants going to work there in 1893. Civil War disturbed the work in 1902 when Colombian rebels seized Bocas; and the readers of the denomination's missionary magazine, the *Missionary Echo*, were regaled with thrilling stories of besieged missionaries. The work later spread farther around the Chiriqui Lagoon into Colombia.[15]

Five years after the 1907 Union, the whole of the Jamaican work was transferred to the Methodist Episcopal Church.

A number of other early overseas enterprises have already been referred to,[16] but the only one of all these remaining in 1845 was Hamburg, where Richard Knight was the first missionary;[17] for years that society's membership did not reach double figures, and the work was closed in 1857 when new shipping regulations in the port made it impossible to carry on.[18]

---

[13] cf. for instance, *Magazine* (1863), pp. 745-6.
[14] Kirsop, *Historic Sketches of Free Methodism*, pp. 81f.
[15] Townsend, Workman, and Eayrs, *New History of Methodism*, II.351.
[16] See pp. 28-9 *supra*. [17] *Minutes* (1838), pp. 11, 19. [18] ibid. (1857), p. 52.

Australia had been suggested as a possible field in 1839 but no preacher was sent until Joseph Townend sailed for Melbourne in May 1851; at the end of 1854 Mark Bradney had joined him, and two more went out in 1857; others went in the following years, but a considerable number soon left the Connexion. Indeed, the story of the Australian mission is a constant story of legal troubles and secessions, ministers and trustees often taking their chapels with them. The magazines record chapels lost to the Wesleyans and regained from the Wesleyans, or chapels that the Wesleyans tried to wrest from the Free Methodists. It is difficult to ascertain at this distance of time exactly what was happening; it certainly was not a case, as it sometimes was at home, of Wesleyan chapels seceding, and then being returned to their legal owners; presumably it was rather a case of Free Methodist ministers and congregations joining the bigger Church. In any case, there was a series of Court actions, and legal costs mounted to £500; for while the Free Methodists won most of the cases in court, their opponent was unable to pay the costs in one important case. In consequence a connexional appeal was issued.[19]

Happily there were some ministers who could ride the storm, chief of whom was Thomas Adams Bayley, who went to Victoria in 1862, allowing Townend to go to Queensland. Ultimately there were scattered missions in Victoria, Queensland, and New South Wales. Tasmania, we have seen, made a fleeting appearance, but was revived again in 1861 when Richard Miller went out. After some time the Australian churches were grouped in two districts, having annual meetings subject to the Assembly; they had indeed asked to have their own independent Assembly in 1859.[20] These two districts were in 1891 constituted the Annual Assemblies of 'Victoria and Tasmania' and 'Queensland and New South Wales', and from January 1892 all ministers became

[19] *Magazine* (1861), pp. 399, 729. These articles are vague as to the precise nature of the cases.
[20] ibid. (1859), p. 487.

F

colonial ministers, subject to the Australian Assemblies. The Australia picture closes in 1902 when a total of 1,875 members joined in the formation of the Australian Methodist Church; a number of churches had previously, 'for convenience of working, joined some branch of the body now amalgamated'.[21]

In 1859 a request was received from seven members in New Zealand for a missionary to be sent them. Though it was decided to send a man straight away,[22] nothing happened till November 1863, when the Foreign Missions Committee determined to respond and opened a mission in Christchurch. After two years the missionary, John Tyerman, left the Connexion, and the fortune of the mission was in the balance till Matthew Baxter went out and established it, in 1868. A succession of other men followed as the mission increased in scope, but the numbers were never very great; and when Methodist Union in New Zealand came about in 1895, Free Methodism contributed 982 members and fourteen ministers, including supernumeraries.

West African Free Methodism dates from the beginning of 1859. Toward the end of the previous year, Robert Eckett had been in communication with a minister in West Africa. As a result of disputes in Rawdon Street Chapel, Sierra Leone, between liberated slaves and natives of the country, the former had left the chapel in 1844, and being the larger body of the two, took to themselves the name that all had originally borne: West African Methodist Society. This body, distinct from the Wesleyans, was already in existence in 1828, though it adopted its name in 1830, under the superintendency of the Rev. D. Coker, a coloured minister ordained in America. After the split, Anthony O'Connor[23] became their General Superintendent; but they felt the need of a white missionary to guide them, and enlisted the help of the Rev. J. Trotter, a minister in the Countess of Huntingdon's Connexion. Mr Trotter felt that their polity was

[21] *Minutes* (1902), p. 97.   [22] *Magazine* (1859), p. 487.
[23] For a notice of O'Connor, see *Magazine* (1861), p. 175.

nearest that of the Free Methodists, and advised them to communicate with that body.[24] Hence Eckett's correspondence.

In January 1859 Eckett was able to report, through the pages of the *Magazine*,[25] that after studying the 1857 Basis of Union, this body had decided to amalgamate with the Free Methodists; they brought into the union 2,300 members and fourteen chapels and preaching places. In response to Eckett's appeal for volunteers, five men offered to go, and Joseph New, then labouring in Holt, was chosen;[26] a valedictory service was held in Russell Street Chapel, Liverpool, on 23rd May 1859, and he sailed the following day.[27] When he and his wife arrived in Sierra Leone, they were the only white people in the churches with which they were associated. New's letters in the magazines of the period give a fascinating picture of mission work in those early days, including a description of a Watch-night Service à l'africaine.

Charles Worboys joined him fifteen months later, and at the close of a further fifteen months (in December 1861) James Brown joined them, having taken a course in the famous Borough Road Training School so that he might spend the bulk of his time in the training of native teachers and catechists; for they saw that in that land, long known as the 'White Man's Grave', it was important to train native agents. Fever struck all the team time and time again, and on 6th August 1862, while Brown was at the point of death, New, who had worn himself out by watching over his colleague, suddenly died. He was twenty-seven years old.[28] By 1864 both his colleagues had return to England through ill-health, though not before Brown had succeeded in establishing a Native Institute.[29] Other men followed, one of whom, John S. Potts, died within four months of his arrival, in June 1866; but William Micklethwaite (1867-74, 1877-9), Thomas Truscott (1881-8), William Vivian (1887-96)

[24] *Magazine* (1860), pp. 374ff; ibid. (1861), p. 175.
[25] op. cit. p. 113.   [26] ibid. p. 288.   [27] ibid. p. 392.
[28] *Magazine* (1862), p. 700.   [29] ibid. (1863), p. 203.

and Charles H. Goodman (1892-8) were able to stay for longer periods. Of Thomas H. Carthew (1883-7) we shall have something to say later. As a result of the foresight of the early missionaries, native ministers were trained, the earliest being W. H. During and W. J. Leigh, both appointed in 1875. Philip Wilson, who had been sold as a slave when a boy and released when the slave ship was captured, served from 1870 to 1881; but he had been a Wesleyan minister before 1870. When Union came about in 1907, only two men on the field were English; there were 2,510 members.

At first the field was restricted to the coastal areas, but in 1882 or early 1883 work was started farther inland among the Mendi people. Their early stations there were destroyed in a native war in 1887, and having been rebuilt were destroyed again in the rising of 1898. In 1892 Vivian decided to concentrate on the Mendi work, and consequently in that year C. H. Goodman, newly out from England, was stationed at Tikonko. There he remained until he was invalided home as a result of a native rising in May 1898. This rising was a protest against the abolition of slavery and the hut tax; and everything British, missionaries and their converts included, were the objects of the Africans' wrath. At Tikonko, John C. Johnson, a native minister, was murdered, as were also Timothy Campbell, the mission school-teacher, and Theo Roberts, the industrial teacher, and other Africans. Goodman took refuge, but after being in hiding some little time, he was betrayed and marched to the rebel headquarters in his pants and vest. Dragged before a council, he saw one man go through a dumb show, the only meaning of which was: 'Death!' Goodman burst out: 'You do not know; you do not reckon upon God!' An old man then pleaded that he should not die, amid murmurs of approval from many; a woman took up his case, clasping King Gruburu's knees; and finally the king said in his broken English: 'You do not fight; you teach the children book; you are kind to all women; you mend people who are sick. That is all good; there is no bad in it;

you shall not be killed. . . . The King will care for you till the war is done.' For days he was kept in a hut in filth and privation, until at last a sub-chief, whom Goodman had nursed some years earlier, brought him clean garments. After three weeks the king panicked, and he and his people fled, taking Goodman with them, now suffering from black-water fever; but happily a native brought him his Bible, helmet and—quinine! No gift could have been more providential. Gruburu's town was destroyed by a punitive expedition, and Goodman's release demanded. Gradually the chiefs sent in their submission, but Gruburu pleaded that he was too ill to travel, and sent his captive, the sick Goodman, as his plenipotentiary to treat with the English forces! Ingenuously, he asked Goodman when he was coming back again. 'If God wills, when the rains are over,' was the reply. Of such stuff were our missions founded! When he finally arrived at the British camp eight weeks after the raid, his sufferings had made such havoc of his health that he was not recognized. The cable telling of his release reached England while the 1898 Assembly was meeting at Lincoln. 'Goodman alive,' read the message; and, says Vivian, strong men were moved to tears, and the Doxology was sung.[30]

By a strange reversal of history, the 'West African Methodist Church', which was the origin of our work in Sierra Leone, seceded in 1934 or 1935 from the newly united Methodist Church, and is again an independent all-African body of some two to three thousand members, as it was a hundred years ago.[31]

East Africa presents the most moving, if not the most successful, stories on the Free Methodist Mission field. The story starts with the publication of *Travels, Researches, and Missionary Labours During an Eighteen Years' Residence in Eastern Africa . . .*' by the Rev. Dr J. Lewis Krapf in 1860. This substantial volume of 556 pages, illustrated with

[30] The full story should be read in William Vivian's *Mendiland Memories* (London n.d., *c.* 1926) and his *A Captive Missionary in Mendiland* (London 1899).
[31] Holt and Clark, *The World Methodist Movement* (Nashville, Tenn., 1956), pp. 133, 145.

maps and lithographs, came into the possession of Charles Cheetham of Heywood, who was at the time a leading layman, and became in 1861 the treasurer of Connexional and Mission Funds. Cheetham saw in this book a call to the UMFC to start mission work in East Africa, and at his own expense invited Krapf to meet the Missionary Committee. So one typical November day in Manchester in 1860 the Committee met Krapf in Lever Street Chapel, and the outcome was a decision by the Committee, which the 1861 Assembly confirmed, that a mission should be started in that field, which Dr Krapf offered to help to establish, though he himself was a missionary of the CMS. Volunteers were asked for, and of eight who offered themselves, Thomas Wakefield and James Woolner were chosen; with them went two young Swiss, Solomon Elliker and Friedrich Graf, who had trained at a missionary-training institution at St Chrischona in Basle. This was of course a time when Africa was 'in the news'; Livingstone, Rebmann, Speke and others were actually at that time pursuing their explorations, and a romantic aura was cast about the very name of Africa. Consequently the Free Methodist public was prepared for the appeals that would be made to support the mission, by a series of articles in the connexional magazine for 1861 on Dr Krapf's life and travels; it was still a time when folk at home listened open-eyed with wonder at travellers' tales.

The two young men, then, left England in June 1861, and after a short stay in Germany, travelled via Trieste to Alexandria. There were no quick flights or direct journeys in those days! It was a question of getting a boat to the next port and hoping for the best when you got there. The voyage, a most trying one, lasted over two months, part of the journey in a rat-infested native boat. Travelling by way of Zanzibar, they finally reached Mombasa on 20th January 1862, Wakefield and Woolner both having suffered seriously from fever. The two young Swiss found conditions more appalling than they could tolerate and very soon returned home. (That sad story has a happy ending. When Wakefield went as a representative to the 1900 Ecumenical Missionary Conference in New York, a gentleman came up to him and said: 'Don't you know *me*?' It was Friedrich Graf, meeting him again after thirty-nine years.[32] It is good to know that one of the two who had left Africa so early later made good.) After a very short time of reconnoitring for the best place to establish the mission, James Woolner became so ill that his immediate return was imperative. Similarly, before the summer was over, having helped to erect a sectional iron house in Ribé, the spot they had chosen, some thirty miles from Mombasa, Krapf also had a breakdown and had to return home. On 7th October 1862 one only of the five was left. Wakefield was twenty-six. By all human standards he could have been pardoned for going home; he had gone as one of five, expecting to have three colleagues of his own generation and one man experienced in life in the tropics, experienced in several of the local languages, and experienced in dealing with the people. He could easily have gone home. But he stayed. And he stayed for twenty-seven years.

In April 1863, Wakefield was joined by Charles New, who, as he had set out to meet the Missionary Committee, had received the news of his brother Joseph's death in Sierra Leone. At the beginning of the following year they were joined by Edmund Butterworth, who reached Mombasa in February 1864 and died on 2nd April. Six weeks and his work was done! In his twenty-seven years of service Wakefield had two furloughs. From his first, he brought back his wife Rebecca; two and a half years later she was dead, leaving him with an infant daughter. It was at this time, too, that he baptized his first converts —twenty-one of them, the fruit of ten years' work. Other missionaries went out, evangelistic and industrial; some died, others were invalided home. Wakefield drowned his sorrows in work, extending the mission in his dream of reaching the Gallas, 'who at the call of the emancipating Saviour, were to leap to the forefront of Africa's peoples,

[32] E. S. Wakefield, *Thomas Wakefield* (London 1904), p. 268.

to lead a nation out of darkness into the light of Christian civilization'.[33] He established stations at Mazeras (so named by the railway company, after Thomas Mazera, a Free Methodist native minister who was stationed there many years), Jomvu, and Golbanti. He finally returned home in 1887, became President the following year, and the next year was elected FRGS. Not his least important work was his translation of parts of the Scriptures into some of the native languages.

Charles New, who had joined him in 1863, for the first twelve months battled for his life against repeated attacks of malaria and dysentery. Not happy at the choice of Ribé as a centre, he failed to see why Swahili traders should reach the tribes of the interior and Christian missionaries should not. He became perforce an explorer, though only that he might extend the mission. He wrote: 'Let me never think of merging the missionary into the traveller! Let me not be the discoverer of lands unknown, except as it may be necessary to the salvation of souls! Not ambition be my guide—but only Thy glory!'[34] But he covered himself, and the Connexion he represented, with glory, for in 1871 he was the first man ever to reach the eternal snows of Kilimanjaro, accompanied at the end only by one faithful servant, Tofiki. Charging straight into work on his return from furlough, during which he wrote his *Life, Wanderings, and Labours in Eastern Africa*,[35] he ran into trouble in the shape of sickness and a mad king assembling his troops for a raid; and before Wakefield could answer his cry for help, he had died. At the time of his death he was the only Corresponding Member of the Royal Geographical Society, apart from Livingstone himself.

Of other men we can only write briefly. But mention must be made of the giant, Thomas Henry Carthew, who after four years in West Africa, spent nine in Kenya.

[33] A. J. Hopkins, *Trail Blazers and Road Makers* (London, n.d., c. 1927), p. 30. This book gives a moving picture of the quiet heroism of the East African pioneers.
[34] S. S. Barton, *Memorials of Charles New* (London 1876), p. 221.
[35] This tells the full story of the ascent of Kilimanjaro.

A giant in strength, he once lifted a chest that four Africans were unable to lift, and carried it to its destination. A giant in heart, he gave of his own meagre resources and lived on native food, in order that he might have money to redeem slaves. He was a giant in resource, too. 'Repeating the Commandments one day in church, according to form, everything went calmly on until they reached number eight. "Thou shalt not steal", thundered Carthew. "Thou shalt not steal," repeated the congregation. There was a pause. "Thou shalt not steal— coconuts," announced Carthew. This was an entirely unexpected innovation, and dead silence reigned. "Say it," demanded the preacher. In hesitating tones came the response. "Thou shalt not steal—coconuts." "Now say this: 'Thou shalt not steal—bananas.' 'Thou shalt not steal—fowls',", and so on mercilessly through the whole programme of their petty pilferings.'[36] Characteristically, he lost his life in answering a cry for help during the night. An accident led to blood-poisoning, and before any colleague could reach him, he had died, on 27th November 1896. He had scorned to take any furlough.

Few events moved the Free Methodists (not even the near massacre of Goodman) as did the murder of John and Annie Houghton. This young couple arrived in Africa in November 1884. In January 1886 they started work at Golbanti where no white woman had ever been before, and set about re-establishing the mission, which had been unoccupied for some months, and rebuilding the chapel. On 3rd May, while Houghton was in the chapel plastering, the wild Masai raided the mission station, and Houghton ran out in time to see his wife struck down, and in a moment he had joined her, transfixed by three spears.[37] Others of the noble army there were too: Matthew Shakala,[38] Robert Moss Ormerod, John Henry Martin, Mrs R. C. Ramshaw, E. W. B.

[36] Hopkins, op. cit. p. 51.

[37] See R. Brewin, *The Martyrs of Golbanti* (London, n.d., c. 1888).

[38] For an account of this native minister, cf. J. H. Phillipson and R. H. B. Shapland, *Tana Talk* (London, n.d., c. 1925), pp. 71ff.

Edmunds, Mrs J. B. Griffiths, Charles Consterdine, J. G. English, William Ernest Northon, W. Udy Bassett; and others were driven back by sickness. 'Their names are names of kings.' That field meant almost certain early death; but the procession went on. One can only stand in amazement—and worship:

> *I ask them, whence their victory came;*
> *They, with united breath,*
> *Ascribe their conquest to the Lamb,*
> *Their triumph to His death.*

The later Methodist history of Kenya, with the entry into Meru, took place after the 1907 union, and so does not concern us here. But the man who was responsible, J. B. Griffiths, went out as early as January 1895, went down with fever every second week, but served at Mazeras from 1896 till his death in 1932. In 1907 there were 404 members in the East Africa District.

East Africa was the first UMFC mission to a purely heathen people; China was their other such field. The indefatigable Robert Eckett raised the question of a mission to China in a letter to the connexional magazine in 1861,[39] having learnt that Hudson Taylor's father had suggested the possibility to James Everett. Eckett thus canvassed support for the project, announcing that one anonymous friend (later acknowledged to be Charles Cheetham) had already promised £200 if the Free Churches would undertake such a mission. The Committee confirmed the proposal, providing the extra income could be raised. Support was immediately obtained in many District Meetings (though there was later some opposition in the 1862 Assembly from the cautious Richard Chew and others), and by January 1862 over £550 had been promised, including £100 from a 'working man'.[40] Again Charles Cheetham took practical steps, and invited Hudson Taylor to meet the Committee that they

---

[39] *Magazine* (1861), pp. 725, 740; ibid. (1862), p. 29.
[40] ibid. (1862), p. 130.

might obtain as much information as possible. Consequently it was decided to send two men to Ningpo, once the Taiping rebellion was over, and Taylor offered to give them previous instruction in the Ningpo dialect. The first man to go was William R. Fuller, recommended by the London Fourth Circuit. He had lessons from Taylor and became a medical student at the London Hospital to make himself the more useful. Thus it was the summer of 1864 before he sailed, tragically losing his youngest child on the voyage. Just before his departure another volunteer came forward in the person of John Mara, who also profited by Hudson Taylor's tutoring. Needless to say, they found they could not preach in the vernacular straight away; a native preacher delivered the address. In 1868 the staff was further strengthened by the accession of Frederick Galpin, who came from the same circuit as Fuller. The health of both Fuller and Mara failed, for Ningpo is no health resort, fever and ague being the fortune of even the most seasoned foreign inhabitants; Fuller consequently tried a change of situation, labouring for a time at Chefoo, but nothing was permanently established there. Mara returned to England in 1869 and Fuller a year later.

This left Galpin alone, and he remained alone for three or four years. Nor was his work in vain; he had conversions in Ningpo and opened one or two new chapels that were crowded from morn till night on the opening day. A number of Chinese preachers helped him, till at length Robert Swallow was sent out in the summer of 1874. In the meantime Galpin's second wife had to go home—and her husband never saw her again. At the 1875 Assembly, the Chinese churches presented a beautifully written address, which thanked the home Church for sending out missionaries, and reported six preaching-stations, thirteen ministers, exhorters and teachers, and a hundred members. The 1877 Assembly appointed Robert Inkerman Exley, of Leeds, who on arrival in China set about establishing work in Wenchow. Unhappily he died after four years. Returning to China after a furlough,

Galpin had charge of this new station as well as Ningpo, until W. E. Soothill went out in 1882. This is the third really great name in Free Methodist work in China. Galpin and Swallow each gave thirty years, Galpin serving later in the home work and becoming President in 1900, Swallow giving up one furlough to study medicine, receiving his doctorate in San Francisco, and also returning to serve in the home work. But seven years later he went out again for a further five years as a medical missionary; in 1897 he too became President. Soothill had a most distinguished career. He wrote a hymn-book, dictionary, and many other books, including a translation of the New Testament into the Wenchow dialect; he later became President of the Imperial University, and then Professor of Chinese at Oxford. His daughter is the writer, Lady Dorothea Hosie.

In 1892 J. W. Heywood started to work in Wenchow, but went to Ningpo four years later, and in all gave forty years to China.

One feature of the Chinese work was the very good colleges that were established in Ningpo and Wenchow, both guided, by a strange coincidence, by sons of Presidents: Herbert S. Redfern, the son of William Redfern, was Principal of Ningpo, and Thomas W. Chapman, the son of Henry T. Chapman, of Wenchow. The first medical missionary as such, Alfred Hogg, went out in 1894 to Wenchow, and two years later the first woman missionary, Miss Emma Hornby, went to serve gratuitously in Ningpo.

The work was hindered by risings from time to time; the property was destroyed on one occasion and commandeered on others. The Boxer Rising in 1900 caused an almost complete cessation of the work; and the current pages of the *Missionary Echo* were filled with stories of heroism and martyrdom. But a great work was done, and the progress in some areas was amazing. The work at Wenchow, for instance, grew from thirty church members, when Soothill went there, to 200 churches, thirty native ministers, nearly 200 local preachers, and a Christian community numbering 10,000—all in twenty-five years!

In the year of Union there were in the China mission a total of 4,118 members with 6,800 on trial.

What of the home support for missions? The early magazines give a vivid picture of an enthusiasm and a generosity that shame us today. At a missionary meeting in Manchester in 1859, 2,000 were present and the collection amounted to £300. The same year the Free Methodists of Blackburn took the Town Hall for a missionary meeting, filled it with 1,500 people, and took over £100. Even a little village like Yatton in the Worle Circuit took £10 at a Juvenile Missionary meeting. The most amazing act of generosity took place on the occasion of the opening of Baillie Street Chapel, Rochdale, when, with the whole cost of the building still to be met, the collections at the opening services, totalling nearly £500, were given to the Home and Foreign Mission Fund.[41]

And all that was in the days when the pound was worth a pound, and incomes were infinitely lower than today. The accounts also tell of a local preacher who gave up smoking in order to be able to give more to missions (*verb. sap.!*), and of individual circuits whose missionary income was over £200 a year. The great days were the days of the May Meetings, when Exeter Hall would be packed to hear the Connexion's 'stars', plus any missionaries who happened to be on furlough; but was there ever a greater galaxy than gathered in Manchester's Lever Street for their Missionary Anniversary in 1862: James Everett, Joseph Garside, William Reed, Samuel Saxon Barton, Joseph Colman, John Guttridge, Richard Chew—every one of them either a past, present, or future President?

A new development in missionary advocacy was the establishment of a monthly magazine, the *Missionary Echo*, in 1894. Originally edited by Joseph Kirsop, this magazine became the missionary organ of the UMC after 1907, and as such continued until 1932.

But perhaps the note that deserves to close this chapter

---

[41] E. C. Cryer, *A Centenary History of the Methodist Church, Baillie Street, Rochdale*, p. 22.

is afforded by Leeds: 'A meeting, of a very interesting and somewhat peculiar character, was held in Lady Lane Chapel, on Monday evening [7th October 1861], *viz.*, a *Missionary Meeting*, without a collection, its object being to give information respecting our Missions, and to induce a spirit of prayer on behalf of them.'[42] Generosity and prayer, then as now, went hand in hand.

[42] *Magazine* (1861), p. 717.

VI

A DREAM COMES TRUE

THE FREE METHODISTS had a veritable passion for Union. Of the seventy-two Assemblies from the beginning of the Wesleyan Association in 1836 till the closing UMFC Assembly of 1907, thirty-two of them (almost half) passed resolutions in favour of union in terms similar to these: 'That the meeting is deeply impressed with the conviction of the desirableness of a union—on New Testament principles—of all the branches of the Methodist Family, and it is an instruction to the Committee now appointed to take into their most serious consideration, and report to the Meeting, what measures can be adopted to effect such a purpose, at the earliest practicable period.'[1] In later years they were sometimes more practical, so to speak, in that they spoke of a union of the various *liberal* Methodist communities.[2] In addition, there were other Assemblies which reported amalgamations, which addressed fraternal greetings to other Methodist bodies, in later years including the Wesleyans, and which referred to other Churches, such as the American Protestant Methodists, with whom they had what they called a 'fraternal union'. In addition, toward the close of the century there were joint bodies and conferences—notably the Ecumenical Methodist Conferences of 1881, 1891, and 1901, and the 'Committee for Methodist Concerted Action'[3]—in which they played their part. This last Committee was concerned with matters that affected the whole Methodist family, and especially the question of 'overlapping' when new chapels were being built. Contrary to what some among us would like us to believe, that concern is *not* the discovery of this enlightened post-1945 era!

[1] *Minutes* (1836), p. 11.   [2] ibid. (1863), p. 58.
[3] cf. the *Minutes* for 1896 onward.

95

Nor were these resolutions academic only—they were often troubled at the academic nature of the replies they received. They meant business.[4] In addition to the resolutions of 1855 and 1856, which bore fruit in the 1857 union, resolutions were passed, either in response to, or as an invitation to, the New Connexion in 1844 (by the WMA), 1863, 1866, and 1889 to 1891.[5]

Robert Eckett had taken the initiative in May 1844 in approaching the New Connexion, but though it met with a warm response from Thomas Allin, speaking for the Conference, nothing came of it.[6] But in 1863 the New Connexion made the first move, Dr Cooke being the leader among that body. Their resolution that year, sent to most of the sister conferences, 'drew forth a cordial response from the Assembly of the UMFC. This denomination has always been alert to respond to friendly approaches, and considering the frequent interchanges of friendly messages and the repeated negotiations for union which have transpired between it and the Methodist New Connexion, it is passing strange that union has not been accomplished between them long ago.'[7] The Assembly went further, and authorized 'the Connexional Committee to confer with any of the liberal Methodist bodies who may be willing to enter into negotiations, with a view to give effect to the preceding resolutions'.[8] Unhappily, to use Townsend's words, this friendly resolution was acknowledged by a 'meaningless academic message' from the New Connexion.[9]

In 1866 Dr Cooke reopened the question in a resolution pointed directly to the Free Methodists; but Dr Stacey enlarged the motion to give it a more general application—

[4] See p. 41, *supra*.

[5] The MNC made a move in 1837 and the Committee was warm in its response; but the Assembly decided that it had conceded too much, especially regarding the functions of Conference. In addition, the Association felt that what the MNC had in mind was not union but absorption; the MNC was to preserve its constitution inviolate. See *Minutes* (1837), pp. 20-1.

[6] cf. *Minutes* (1844), pp. 27ff.

[7] W. J. Townsend, *Story of Methodist Union*, p. 94.

[8] *Minutes* (1863), p. 58.   [9] op. cit. p. 95.

and therefore a less definite one. Thus it was addressed to the Wesleyans as well as to the other Connexions, Samuel Hulme, the New Connexion President, accompanying it with an explanatory letter. A phrase in his letter to the Wesleyans occasioned some surprise, and, not unnaturally, some distrust on the part of the Free Methodists; he prayed that the time would soon come when they 'the first exiles, may "come again to our Father's house in peace" '.[10] This letter was reprinted in the Free Methodist Magazine of 1866; it was accompanied by an editorial comment by William Reed: 'On behalf of the United Methodist Free Churches, we venture to affirm that, whatever may be the case with other Methodist "exiles", they have no passionate yearnings after their "father's house", as Mr Hulme designates the Conference Community. When its leaders cease to act "as Lords over God's heritage", and manifest a desire for reunion with those whom they have grievously injured, we will be glad to aid them in the good work.'[11]

Yet they were ready to discuss union with the 'liberal Methodists', and stated that they believed 'that the time has fully come when a more practical issue should be attempted'.[12] Consequently, at the suggestion of the Free Methodists, a conference was held in Leeds in May 1867, which appointed sub-committees to deal with the practical difficulties arising from the Deed Poll of the New Connexion and the UMFC Foundation Deed. Those sub-committees never met.[13] Both conferences in 1867 confirmed what had been done so far, but the 1868 New Connexion Conference brought the negotiations to an end by a resolution which commended 'the practical issue to the great Head of the Church'.[14]

Twenty years passed. Then in 1886 Hugh Price Hughes raised the question of union between the Wesleyans and the New Connexion; this finally, after a promising start,

[10] Townsend, *Story of Methodist Union*, p. 99; *Magazine* (1866), p. 616.
[11] op. cit. pp. 615-16.   [12] *Minutes* (1866), p. 67.
[13] Townsend, op. cit. p. 108; Kirsop, *Historic Sketches of Free Methodism*, p. 59.
[14] Townsend, ibid. p. 110.

petered out in generalizations,[15] but it reopened the question of union among the other bodies. Then as a result of a chance conversation between Marmaduke Miller of the Free Methodists and Dr Townsend, an informal meeting took place in Dr Townsend's house between representative men of the two denominations; this led to a statesmanlike article by Miller in the UMFC *Magazine* of May 1888, a move from the UMFC Connexional Committee, and a resolution from the 1888 Assembly that was more cautious in its wording than some had been.[16] The matter was further taken up in the magazines of the two bodies, and both in their 1889 Conferences decided to set up a joint committee. This met on four occasions in the course of the next twelve months and drafted a scheme of union. But in the New Connexion Conference of 1890 there was a strong body of opposition, and a smaller group in the Free Methodist Assembly. The New Connexion decided to submit one or two questions regarding the position of the Ministry to the consideration of the UMFC, but this was really an attempt to cover up a real cleavage of opinion among both ministers and members. The Free Methodist reply was unhappily regarded as evasive, with the result that the 1891 Conference decided that further action was at the moment inadvisable. The Free Methodists could only courteously accept the decision.[17]

The movement that finally led to union in 1907 began with the 1901 Ecumenical Conference. Indeed, it may be said to have begun with the first such conference in 1881, which drew the Methodist Churches together, and especially with a dramatic event there. William Griffith was not a keen supporter of the Conference. 'He feared it would be a meaningless piece of acting, covered with a thin veneer of courtesy, but without cordial feeling.'[18] He allowed himself to be elected as a representative, however, and, once there, changed his mind. 'It was a great

---

[15] Townsend, ibid. pp. 146ff.   [16] *Minutes* (1888), p. 163.
[17] cf. Townsend, *Story of Methodist Union*, pp. 163ff.; *Minutes* (1889), p. 172; (1890), p. 201; (1891), p. 187.
[18] R. Chew, *William Griffith, Memorials and Letters* (London 1885), p. 223.

success—a success of hallowed and fraternal meetings.'[19]
But let Griffith himself tell the story.

'At an early sitting, while listening attentively to a
matter before the Conference, I was distracted by a
bustling noise behind me from one who was saying in
earnest but suppressed tones: "I must shake hands with
him, I must shake hands with him." Turning round to
see who was causing this disturbance, the person stretched
out his hand eagerly saying: "Griffith, let me shake hands
with you." Putting out mine, he gave me a most vigorous
shake; and this I returned quite heartily also. Still
retaining each other's hand, I said: "I do not know you.
Who are you?" "Don't you know me?" "No; I never saw
you in my life, as far as I recollect. What is your name?"
"Hargreaves." "Hargreaves?" I responded. And after a
short pause, recollecting the name, I asked: "What!
Joseph Hargreaves?" "Yes." "The Joseph Hargreaves
who, with George Osborn and Henry Chettle, of your
own head issued that test circular that caused my expulsion?" "The very same; but I most heartily shake hands
with you, and am very glad to see you here, as are all my
brethren." "And I as heartily shake hands with you." '[20]

But on the third day of the 1901 Conference, Dr T. B.
Stephenson declared that they had 'reached the point at
which any serious further advance spells *union* and nothing
else'.[21] The younger Churches responded warmly, but no
response in the Conference came from Stephenson's own
Church. Thereupon Dr David Brook, then President of
the UMFC, together with one of his leading laymen, Mr
Robert Bird, of Cardiff, invited leading men of the New
Connexion, the Bible Christians, and his own Church—
the three Churches that had always been the most
determined to do something—to lunch at the National
Liberal Club, and it was resolved after some informal
conversation to make a real effort toward union of the
three Churches. The matter came of course before the

[19] ibid. p. 225.
[20] Letter to an old friend, Mrs Hart, quoted in Chew, op. cit. pp. 226-7.
[21] Townsend, op. cit. p. 135.

annual gatherings of all the Methodist Churches in 1902, and four (the above three with the Wesleyan Reform Union) passed resolutions empowering their executive committees to confer with their 'opposite numbers'.

Meetings of representatives took place on 18th December 1902 and 6th March 1903, at which the Reform Union was represented, and a tentative basis of union was drawn up. Hope was not yet given up that an even wider union might be possible, and the other Conferences were in consequence approached. It has been said somewhere (and if it is true, it is to their honour) that the reason the Primitive Methodists did not join in the negotiations was that their connexional finances were in a bad state, and they did not want to embarrass the new community in that way. The Wesleyans voted simply to inquire into the conditions and relations of the Churches desiring union, but not to consider union themselves;[22] and when the Wesleyan representatives met the joint committee in December 1903 it was evident that the Wesleyan insistence on the Pastoral Conference was going to prove an insurmountable barrier.[23] Consequently the other three Churches (the Wesleyan Reform Union having withdrawn) continued to draft a constitution. They had been encouraged by the answers of the Quarterly Meetings of the three bodies to two questions:

(1) Do you approve of union with the above-named Churches, or other Methodist Churches, if found practicable?
(2) Do you approve of an effort being made by duly appointed representatives, with representatives of other Churches, to draft a Constitution, such Constitution to be afterwards submitted to the Quarterly Meetings and the Conference?[24]

There was an amazing unanimity in the voting, the Bible Christians giving the greatest support of all. But summing it up, there was a 93 per cent vote for the

---

[22] Townsend, ibid. p. 225.

[23] The conditions, and the Wesleyan reactions, are found in *Wesleyan Minutes* (1904), pp. 535ff.

[24] Townsend, op. cit. p. 222.

onward movement;[25] and the Conferences of the three communities could therefore confirm the action of the joint committee and instruct it to prepare the main outlines of a constitution. The sense of oneness among the three bodies had no doubt been developed by the fact that the *Free Methodist*, the weekly paper of the UMFC, from October 1902 became also the weekly organ of the New Connexion and the Bible Christians, as well as of the UMFC.

At this point, the Wesleyan Conference took a regrettable step. As an amendment to a motion blessing the efforts of the three Churches, Mr (as he then was) R. W. Perks, M.P., moved that the Wesleyan Church should approach the New Connexion with a view to a union between them. This could only be interpreted as a deliberate attempt to prevent the union that was being negotiated, and as such it was vigorously opposed by Dr J. S. Simon, Mr (later Sir) Percy Bunting, and Dr J. H. Rigg, who remarked that to 'appoint a committee now, when the New Connexion had not approached them, was a shabby proceeding; it was an altogether unworthy proceeding; undignified was a far too light epithet to apply to a proceeding like that'.[26] But the amendment was nevertheless carried. The New Connexion replied in a long and dignified resolution, that was at the same time loyal to its fellow-negotiators and courteous toward the Wesleyan Conference. It twice addressed the Conference as 'Honoured Fathers and Brethren', and 'rejoiced in the prosperity of the Wesleyan Methodist Church at home and abroad. It would assure [the] Conference of its filial esteem and reverence'; but was quite firm in its inability to break faith with the Bible Christians and the Free Methodists. 'The invitation proffered is contingent upon our being "free" to accept it,' they said; 'it being

25 The exact figures are to be found in Townsend, ibid. p. 228.
26 ibid. p. 235. The move bore a strange resemblance to the Anglican invitation to Methodism in 1955, when the other Free Churches had been previously engaged with Methodism in the 'conversations'. Unhappily, Methodism then allowed herself to be singled out—dishonourably, as it seemed, and still seems, to the writer.

well known that we have been in negotiation for union with other Methodist Churches for nearly three years. Such being the case, it is clear to us that we are "free" to entertain other proposals only when it has been proved impracticable to effect union with those Churches with which we are now in conference.'[27]

The Assembly met in Rochdale in July 1905 and dealt with the details of the proposed constitution one by one. There was an amendment to the proposed ministerial chairmanship of all meetings, to the effect that 'each meeting shall elect its own chairman'. This of course was an old Free Methodist principle which it was proposed to give up for the sake of union, the more easily as the new proposal was already the normal practice though not the rule; an echo of old battles was heard, in that one of those who supported the amendment was Walter Kaye Dunn, the great-nephew of Samuel Dunn. But the amendment was overwhelmingly defeated.

When the proposals came before the Quarterly Meetings, again there was the same overwhelming vote for the final constitution and the financial arrangements as there had been for the original principle, though as was to be expected there was a larger hostile vote among the Free Methodists than among the others: 97 per cent in the New Connexion voted for the constitution, as against 92 per cent in the Bible Christians and 86 per cent in the Free Methodists; this in part, no doubt, to be accounted for by the fact that ministerial chairmanship had been the rule among the former two bodies, so that on that important issue it was the Free Methodists who were surrendering a point. (But the surrender was more apparent than real; for a layman could henceforward take the chair if the minister were not present; the meeting was still legal.) Their actual figures were: for the Constitution, 4,782 in favour, 253 against, and 202 neutral; for the financial arrangements, 4,249 in favour, 594 against, and 209 neutral.[28] Only two Free Methodist circuits voted

[27] *MNC Minutes* (1905), pp. 34-5.
[28] *Minutes* (1906), p. 325.

against union,[29] and when union took place, only one circuit seceded—and that returned to the fold three years later.[30]

It would not be fitting to close this chapter without a reference to the Uniting Conference. The Assembly normally concluded with the resolution, 'That this Annual Assembly be now dissolved'; but on 16th July 1907, the resolution in Prudhoe Street Chapel, Newcastle-on-Tyne, ran: 'That in harmony with the resolution previously adopted, this Assembly does now adjourn to Wesley's Chapel, City Road, London, on 17th September 1907, at ten a.m.' Consequently at 5.40 in the morning of 17th September, people were beginning to queue for the all-too-few seats in the historic chapel lent for the occasion. There were those there who had been at the previous Uniting Assembly fifty years earlier, such as J. Swann Withington, who had entered the Ministry sixty-five years previously, and Edward Boaden, who was to be elected President, and who had entered the Ministry in the year of the last disruption in 1849.

One by one the Presidents and Secretaries of the three uniting bodies took their places on the platform, followed later by distinguished visitors summoned from the gallery of the chapel. W. B. Lark, the oldest of the three Presidents, announced the Doxology, and then followed 'My heart and voice I raise.' One wonders if the popularity of that hymn in the old United Methodist Church was in part due to that hallowed association. After prayers and words of welcome, the venerable Edward Boaden was nominated as President by John S. Clemens of the New Connexion and John B. Stedeford of the Bible Christians. The election was unanimous, as were those of George Packer of the New Connexion as Secretary and John Luke of the Bible Christians as Conference Minutes Secretary.

The new insignia of office were then presented, consisting of a President's gavel, bearing the significant

[29] Townsend, op. cit. p. 253.

[30] Smith, Swallow, and Treffry, *The Story of the U.M. Church* (London, n.d. [1932]), p. 25.

inscription, '*Primus inter Pares*', contained in a silver casket which also enclosed the President's Bible and a copy of John's Gospel in all the languages spoken where the three Churches had missions.

The resolution on union was then put to all the three Churches in turn and finally to the United Conference, and on each occasion was carried unanimously. In the same way the Deed of Foundation was adopted, as also the Model Trust Deed. The sense of real union was also shown later when the twenty-four Guardian Representatives were to be elected. As the Free Methodists contributed 54 per cent of the uniting membership, they could by right have claimed that more than half of these twenty-four should be theirs. But they said: 'No; let eight belonging to the New Connexion Church be elected and eight belonging to the Bible Christian Church and eight belonging to ours.'[31] In the same way was the Connexional Committee elected; by a strange coincidence—or the working of Providence among those who were showing His spirit—of the first nine freely elected Presidents, three were from each of the three Churches. In such a way is a real union formed. Many more unions would have been more effective if the same generous principles had been adopted by the major party.

The new Church was, in conclusion, a *Methodist* Church —and demonstrated its concern with its primary purpose —'to save souls'—by holding a 'Simultaneous Mission' in the spring of the following year, when 5,000 decisions for Christ were registered.

[31] ibid. p. 12. The whole story of that Uniting Conference is movingly told in this volume.

VII

POSTSCRIPT

We have called our sketch 'A Study in Freedom'. We have tried to trace the history, the principles, the ways, of a Connexion which believed that a Church is strongest when the greatest number of people play an effective part in its life, and when the greatest amount of devolution takes place in the government of its affairs. The UMFC experimented in freedom. Theoretically, they seemed to be a loose confederacy, and their critics called them 'a rope of sand'; but because the connexional loyalty was voluntary and not imposed, it was all the stronger. It had indeed something of the spirit of the British Commonwealth of Nations, whose sole bond is a common loyalty to the Sovereign, but whose loyalty to one another is none the less real. It had the spirit of an adult family, the members of which are independently responsible for making their own way in the world, but who remain bonded together by unbreakable ties. We lose that spirit at our peril.

MINUTES,

&c., &c.

1. The proceedings of the Twenty-second Annual Assembly of the Wesleyan Methodist Association, and of the Representatives belonging to the Methodist Reform Circuits, which have consented to the Basis of Union adopted for amalgamating the Churches of the Wesleyan Methodist Association, and the Methodist Reform Churches, the sittings of which commenced on Wednesday, the 29th day of July, in Baillie Street Chapel, Rochdale, and were continued until the 10th of August, 1857.

2. The Rev. M. Baxter, President of the preceding Annual Assembly, opened the Meeting with devotional exercises. After which the list of the Circuits entitled to send Representatives was called over, and the certificates of their appointment were examined by the Connexional Officers, according to the provisions of the Foundation Deed.

3. After the certificates of persons claiming to be Representatives had been examined, several cases which were deemed doubtful, or irregular, were brought under the consideration of those brethren whose certificates had been declared satisfactory. It was then

4. *Resolved,*—That under the present peculiar circumstances in which this Assembly has been convened, the Rev. James Everett, who is resident at Newcastle-on-Tyne, but has been elected to represent the Diss Circuit, be acknowledged as the Representative from that Circuit to this Assembly.

5. *Resolved,*—That as the Great Horton Circuit of Methodist Reformers has not yet consented to the Basis of Union for amalgamating the Churches of the Wesleyan Methodist Association and the Methodist Reformers, the

A 2

FIRST PAGE OF THE MINUTES OF THE FIRST ASSEMBLY OF THE UNITED METHODIST FREE CHURCHES, ROCHDALE, 1857

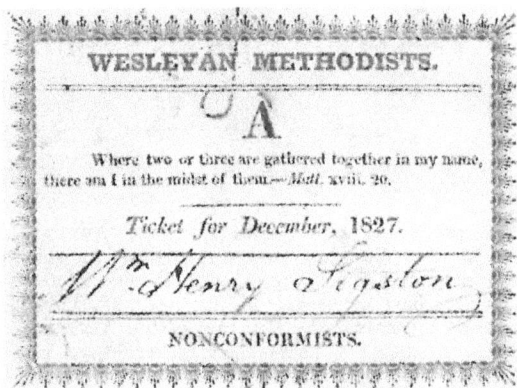

FIRST CLASS-TICKET OF THE PROTESTANT
METHODISTS

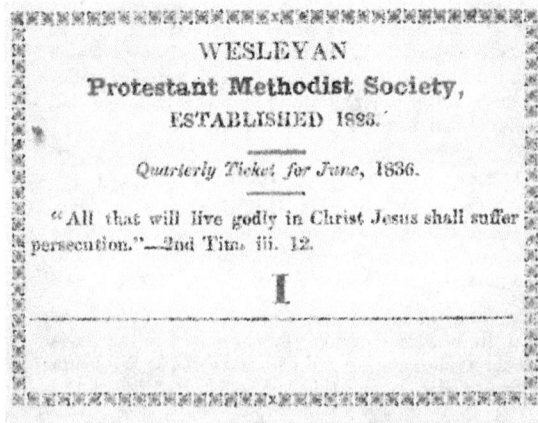

ONE OF THE LAST OF THE PROTESTANT
METHODIST TICKETS

SAMUEL WARREN, LL.D.
President of the Wesleyan Association Assembly, 1836

MINUTES

OF THE

ANNUAL ASSEMBLY

OF

THE DELEGATES

OF THE

WESLEYAN ASSOCIATION,

BEGUN IN MANCHESTER ON WEDNESDAY,
AUGUST 3, 1836.

LONDON :
PUBLISHED BY SIMPKIN, MARSHALL, AND CO.
3, STATIONERS' HALL COURT,
Also to be had at the TABERNACLE, Stephenson Square,
Manchester.

MDCCCXXXVI.

TITLE-PAGE OF FIRST WESLEYAN ASSOCIATION MINUTES,
1836

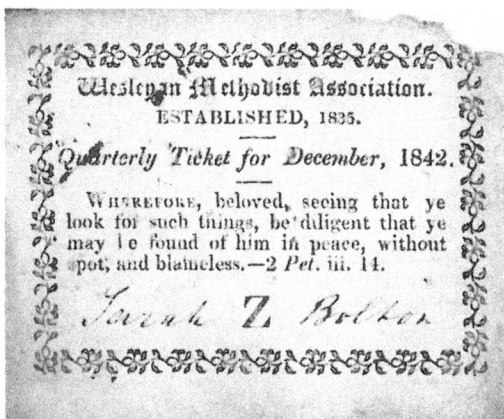

TYPICAL CLASS-TICKET OF THE WESLEYAN
METHODIST ASSOCIATION

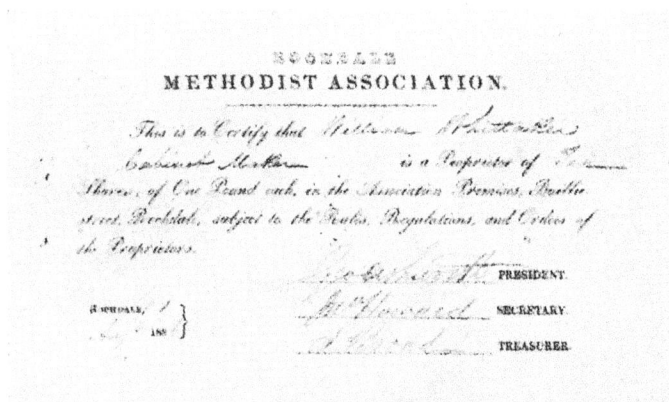

SHARE CERTIFICATE OF BAILLIE STREET CHAPEL,
ROCHDALE, 1836

MATTHEW BAXTER
b. 1812; 1836-93

President of WMA, 1856
Missionary to Jamaica, 1841-51
Missionary to New Zealand, 1868-73

ROBERT ECKETT
b. 1797; 1838-62

President of WMA, 1841, 1846, 1847
President of UMFC, 1858

JAMES EVERETT
b. 1784; 1807-72
President of UMFC, 1857

WILLIAM GRIFFITHS
b. 1806; 1828-83

Elected President of
UMFC, 1877, but
declined to serve

BAILLIE STREET CHAPEL, ROCHDALE
as it was before the alterations made in 1912

HYMN BOOK

OF THE

United Methodist Free Churches,

COMPRISING THE

COLLECTION OF HYMNS

BY

THE REV. JOHN WESLEY, A.M.,

Sometime Fellow of Lincoln College, Oxford.

WITH MISCELLANEOUS HYMNS SUITED FOR OCCASIONAL
SERVICES.

LONDON:

PUBLISHED BY WILLIAM REED,
UNITED METHODIST FREE CHURCHES' BOOK-ROOM,
15, CREED LANE, LUDGATE STREET.
1863.

THE FAMILIAR ENGRAVING OF JOHN WESLEY FACED
THIS PAGE

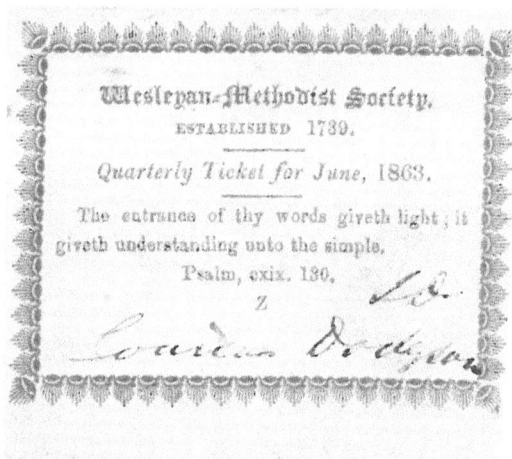

Wesleyan-Methodist Society.

ESTABLISHED 1739.

Quarterly Ticket for June, 1863.

The entrance of thy words giveth light; it giveth understanding unto the simple.

Psalm, cxix. 130.

Z

CLASS-TICKET OF THE WESLEYAN
REFORMERS, 1863
The words 'Wesleyan Reform Union' first appeared in
1865

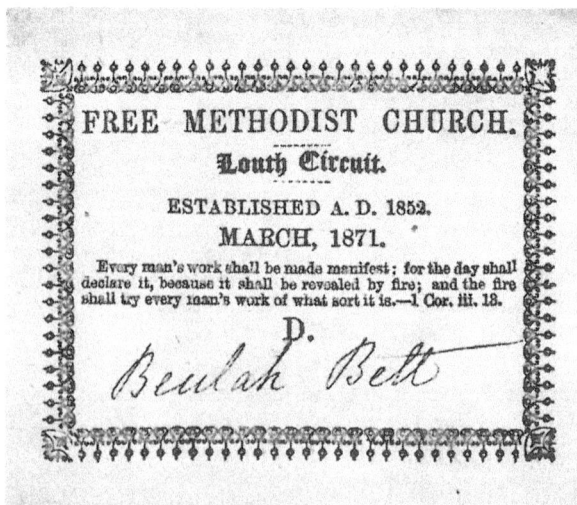

FREE METHODIST CHURCH.

Louth Circuit.

ESTABLISHED A. D. 1852.

MARCH, 1871.

Every man's work shall be made manifest: for the day shall
declare it, because it shall be revealed by fire; and the fire
shall try every man's work of what sort it is.—1 Cor. iii. 13.

D.

TICKET ISSUED BY AN INDEPENDENT CIRCUIT OF
REFORMERS IN 1871

SIR JAMES DUCKWORTH
1840-1915
One of the two
Lay Presidents

EDWARD BOADEN
b. 1827; 1849-1913
President of UMFC, 1871
President of UMC, 1907

WILLIAM VIVIAN
b. 1858; 1880-1926
Missionary in West Africa, 1887-96

CHARLES HENRY GOODMAN
b. 1854; 1889-1939
Missionary in West Africa, 1889-1901

THOMAS WAKEFIELD
b. 1836; 1858-1901

Missionary in East Africa,
1861-87
President of UMFC, 1888

CHARLES NEW
b. 1840; 1860-75

Missionary in East Africa,
1862-75

FREDERICK GALPIN
Missionary in China, 1867-97
President of UMFC, 1900

WILLIAM EDWARD SOOTHILL
b. 1861; 1882-1935
Missionary in China, 1882-1912

THE CIRCUITS OF THE UMFC IN 1857
Each dot represents a circuit; the numbers by some dots represent the
number of circuits in the same town (e.g. 6 in London). Cf. map overleaf

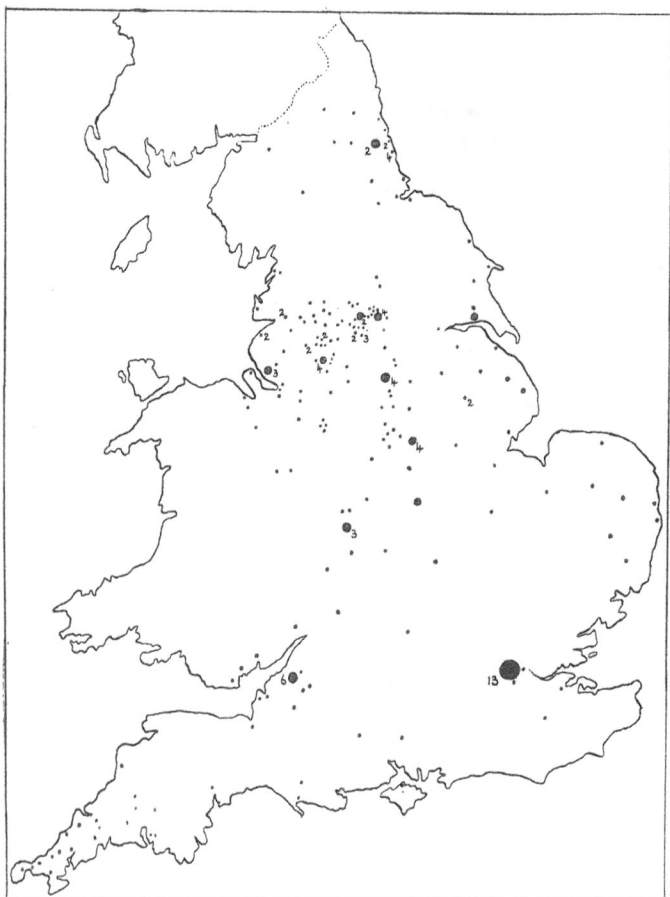

THE CIRCUITS OF THE UMFC IN 1907

INDEX